AWESOME ARIZONA PLACES FOR CURIOUS KIDS

Text and Photography by
Diane T. Liggett and James A. Mack

WESTCLIFFE PUBLISHERS

westcliffepublishers.com

International Standard Book Numbers:
ISBN-10: 1-56579-523-7
ISBN-13: 978-1-56579-523-5

Editor: Kelly Kordes Anton
Design: Graphic Advantage, Ltd.
Design Concept: Mark Mulvany
Production Manager: Craig Keyzer

Published by: Westcliffe Publishers, Inc.
P.O. Box 1261
Englewood, Colorado 80150
westcliffepublishers.com

Printed in China through: World Print, Ltd.

Library of Congress Cataloging-in-Publication Data:
Liggett, Diane T., 1960–
    Awesome Arizona places for curious kids / text and photography by Diane T. Liggett
and James A. Mack
        p. cm.
    Includes bibliographical references and index.
    ISBN-13: 978-1-56579-523-5
    ISBN-10: 1-56579-523-7
  1. Arizona—Description and travel—Juvenile literature. 2. Arizona—History,
Local—Juvenile literature. 3. Parks—Arizona—Juvenile literature. 4. Monuments
—Arizona—Juvenile literature. 5. Historic sites—Arizona—Juvenile literature.
6. Children—Travel—Arizona—Juvenile literature. 7. Family recreation—Arizona
—Juvenile literature.   I. Mack, James A.   II. Title.
    F811.3.L54 2005
    979.1—dc22   2004028340

*For more information about other fine books and calendars from Westcliffe Publishers,
please contact your local bookstore, call us at 1-800-523-3692, write for our free color
catalog, or visit us on the Web at* **westcliffepublishers.com.**

Please Note: Risk is always a factor in backcountry and high-mountain travel.
Many of the activities described in this book can be dangerous, especially when
weather is adverse or unpredictable, and when unforeseen events or conditions
create a hazardous situation. The authors have done their best to provide the
reader with accurate information about backcountry travel, as well as to point
out some of its potential hazards. It is the responsibility of the users of this guide
to learn the necessary skills for safe backcountry travel, and to exercise caution
in potentially hazardous areas. The authors and publisher disclaim any liability
for injury or other damage caused by backcountry traveling or performing any
other activity described in this book.

Cover Photos (clockwise from top left): *Stately saguaro cactus abound in Saguaro
National Park; a Navajo family explores the depths of Canyon de Chelly National
Monument; colorful canyon walls make for an unforgettable trip on the Verde Canyon
Railroad; a young astronomer explores the universe through a telescope at Kitt Peak
National Observatory.*

Opposite: *Hikers on the North Kaibab Trail enjoy the cool temperatures and forested
views of Grand Canyon National Park's North Rim.*

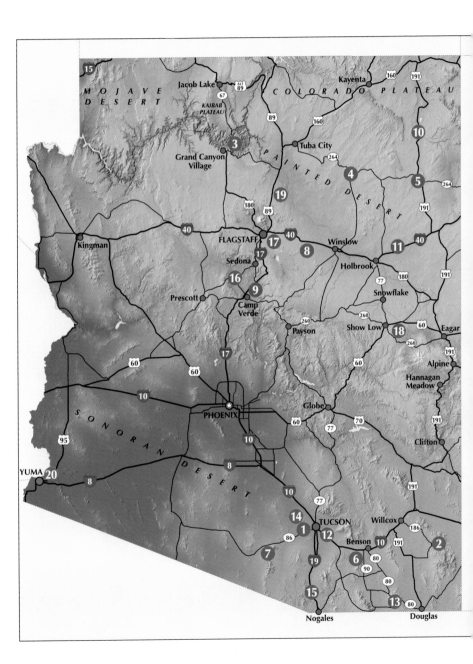

Contents

Part of the Pima Air & Space Museum, the Challenger Learning Center offers several simulated missions into space. Here a flight director is assisting a student during a simulation at Mission Control's Life Support Station.

photo courtesy of Pima Air & Space Museum

Working with professional astronomers, participants in the Nightly Observing Program use telescopes to locate distant planets, stars, galaxies, and nebulae at Kitt Peak National Observatory.

photo courtesy of Robert Wilson
NOAO/AURA/NSF

Lush meadows and dense forests on the North Rim of the Grand Canyon provide important habitat for a variety of wildlife including mule deer, mountain lions, and turkeys. The North Rim, with its lush forests, is a big contrast to the arid desert of the South Rim on the opposite side of Grand Canyon National Park.

Delicate formations decorate the pristine underground world of Kartchner Caverns. Formed over very long periods of time, these formations come in a wide variety of shapes and sizes. The caverns are also home to a colony of bats.

photo courtesy of Arizona State Parks

In the Verde Valley, open-air cars on the Verde Canyon Railroad allow passengers to be surrounded by Nature's sights and sounds. Following the Verde River and traveling through steep-walled canyons, this scenic trip is fun for the entire family. You might even see an eagle!

photo courtesy of Verde Canyon Railroad

In rugged Navajo country, soaring sandstone cliffs surround visitors as they cross a bridge in Canyon del Muerto at Canyon de Chelly National Monument. Guided trips through the monument reveal captivating stories about the cultures that built dwellings more than 1,000 years ago, and the Navajo people who continue to live and farm there today.

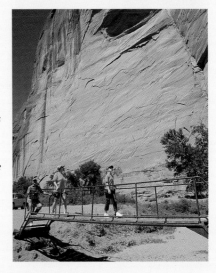

Introduction

This book, *Awesome Arizona Places for Curious Kids,* sends you to some of the most authentic, significant, and awe-inspiring places in Arizona. Each chapter offers intriguing information for explorers with a variety of interests, from history to wildlife watching. You can learn about prehistoric cultures before you visit where they once lived. Before you go on a hike, you can get tips on where to observe secretive animals. You might even want to act as a guide for the rest of your family on your trip!

The most important ingredient for a successful family adventure is imagination. Spend a few minutes with this book before heading off on your journeys, so you can arrive prepared to inspire one another with ideas for making the past seem like the present or the landscape come alive. Each destination has a tale to tell—and sometimes those stories lie just beneath the surface. With the right amount of insight, your imagination may run wild, so it doesn't hurt to have a few answers ahead of time!

Your entire family will discover more about Arizona when you set out on a learning adventure together. Special and unique places such as Walnut Canyon or the White Mountains often exist at the heart of family memories and traditions. Their names alone can trigger reminders of youthful enthusiasm, discovery, and fun. Many families continue to return to destinations such as the Chiricahuas to recapture the spirit and the warmth of those moments. Others refresh their spirits and create more memories by discovering new places.

Arizona is a geologically rich and interesting state. As appropriate, we have identified individual rocks or gemstones that you may wish to collect on your travels, as a reminder of your visit, to start a new hobby, or even to launch a career. With your collection, you can assemble a geographic "snapshot" of Arizona. Keep in mind that it is best to obtain your specimens from local or regional rock shops. It is against the law to collect objects of any type in all national park areas, and often these restrictions apply to other public lands, so always ask about regulations.

Use this family adventure guide to explore 20 destinations in Arizona that possess a powerful sense of place with something for everyone, including everything you need to build unforgettable memories. We wish you happy explorations and many happy memories, both new and old.

Diane T. Liggett and James A. Mack

An Apache camp along the trail to Fort Bowie National Historic Site features a thatched wickiup and a ramada used for shade from the hot summer sun.

Visitors descend a series of 240 steps to view the prehistoric dwellings of Walnut Canyon National Monument. The canyon was once home to the Sinagua people.

Definition of Symbols

Discovery Zone

Each awesome place in Arizona is a discovery zone for amazing facts, fun, excitement, and astonishment. In this section, you'll find out about the most interesting things to see and do in the state. Everything is included—from a visit to the far reaches of the universe at Kitt Peak National Observatory to the depths of the earth at Kartchner Caverns State Park.

Paleo Scene

Arizona is rich in fossil discoveries and ancient secrets in stone. At these scenes, you'll find out about places where paleontology is the main attraction. At Petrified Forest National Park, for example, you can walk among fallen giants from a 200-million-year-old forest. You'll have the chance to apply a hammer and chisel to solid rock, looking for clues to prehistory, at the Arizona-Sonora Desert Museum. Each destination allows for a peek into the past.

Crypto Scene

There is no way to learn all the secrets of Arizona's awesome places. Almost every destination offers some cryptic or hidden puzzles to solve. This section reveals little-known stories, such as training for a space shuttle mission at the Pima Air & Space Museum, talking with ground control, and running experiments. You might even be able to identify fragments of meteorites or start a rock collection that represents all your visits to places of interest around the state.

Wild Things

From fleet-footed pronghorn at Wupatki National Monument to soaring condors at the Grand Canyon, Arizona is one of the wildest places around! You'll encounter wildlife in every corner of the state—and just in case you miss the more elusive species, such as the Mexican gray wolf, the Arizona-Sonora Desert Museum will help you catch that rare glimpse.

Micro Scape

A world of wonder sometimes rests right at your feet—or just beyond your direct line of sight. Take a look at, under, and into some of the smallest or unique things in Arizona.

Back in Time Line

Imagine walking on a path traveled thousands of years ago by people who later vanished! This section reveals the extensive human history of Arizona. From the 1,000-year-old cliff dwellings at Navajo National Monument to the four-story pueblo at Wupatki National Monument, Arizona was populated long before western civilization entered the Southwest. You'll become a time traveler once you get a taste of the state's fascinating past.

Travel Log

In this section of each chapter, you will find the most important information for enjoying your excursions. Directions, important gear to carry, addresses, campground locations, and safety precautions will help you and your family gear up for a successful adventure. Arizona's awesome places are just waiting for you, so find a good map before you hit the road and get ready to encounter the unexpected.

1 Arizona-Sonora Desert Museum

Discovery Zone

"Hey! Is that real?" "No, that can't be real; it hasn't moved." "Wait a minute, I think I just saw it move. It *is* real!" You barely arrive at the Desert Museum when you become spellbound by the clever combination of living things and replicas. Greet an iguana or a Gila monster as it sits motionless on a rock, and examine the detail in sculpted likenesses of other lizards around the sunny enclosure. Follow the snaking sidewalk to the museum entrance past a herd of peccaries cast in bronze. You are about to enter a land of double takes, where exhibits merge with living organisms to re-create one of the most interesting environments in the world—the diverse Sonoran Desert of Arizona, California, Baja California, and Mexico.

Along the self-guided trail, trickling water invites you into the cool darkness of an artificial limestone cave where a dank, narrow detour provides passage for smaller visitors. Low lighting and twisting chambers lined with model bats lead you to displays of underground pools and shimmering cave formations on your way to a sparkling exhibit of regional gems and minerals. "Whoa! Look!" exclaims a boy as he peers through a glass case at some colorful crystals. "These agates look like they have pictures in them!" Such an impressive scene of precious stones could easily occupy you for hours, but more surprises lie ahead as you venture back into the bright desert light.

Rooms With a View

Take a peek through a secret window as you round the bend toward the Mountain Woodland. You may find yourself only inches away from a 125-pound mountain lion resting in the shade, unaware of your presence! This feline predator usually lives in secluded canyon and mountain areas, which are expertly re-created here as realistic habitats. Even the brawny black bear resting on its back seems satisfied by the natural look and feel of the surroundings. Trotting down a well-worn path along a rocky ravine, a pair of Mexican wolves gives visitors a glimpse of an endangered species that has begun a comeback in the wild, thanks in part to a captive breeding program at the Desert Museum.

Underground viewing stations are definitely the highlight of Desert Grasslands, Cat Canyon, Life Underground, and the Riparian Corridor. Explore the lower levels of these natural-looking habitats, and discover how desert

The landscape in the cactus and pollination gardens at the Desert Museum is anything but dull. Spiny plants range from not-so-cuddly teddy bear chollas to mysterious night-blooming cereus, while colorful bird-of-paradise flowers attract hummingbirds, bees, and butterflies.

Lifelike bronze figures appear throughout the grounds of the Desert Museum. These collared peccaries at the museum entrance are some of the first to greet visitors as they begin their excursion into the Sonoran Desert.

Lots of sand and plenty of tools in the Desert Museum's paleontology exhibit provide a hands-on opportunity to understand the excavation process. Patience is an important requirement for future scientists who want to unearth replica fossils at the foot of the cliff.

animals escape daytime heat as well as aboveground predators. Observation windows let you witness the inner workings of a prairie dog town or spy on an elusive ocelot as it naps unknowingly close to your nose. Along the upper reaches of the streamside, or *riparian,* environment you may meet the mascot of the Desert Museum Kid's Club—the curious coati. Peering through a secret porthole as a coati curls its fluffy tail, someone remarks, "Check out that snoot!" Long-nosed relatives of raccoons, these nimble tree-climbers forage high and low for fruit and insects. Continue on to the underwater world of fish and otters, and look for tiny imitation tadpoles speckling the sidewalk. Part of an exhibit on the life cycle of desert toads, these bronze swimmers turn into adults on the other side of the bridge!

Beyond the bighorn sheep, turkey vultures, and attention-grabbing gardens waits one of the most memorable spaces at the Desert Museum. Abandon your binoculars, because action in the Hummingbird Aviary happens so fast, you cannot even catch it with a camera! Rocketing by at speeds up to 45 miles an hour, these desert dive-bombers whir around from feeder to feeder, defending their territories with dazzling displays of sound and color, even though many of the birds have mended from injuries received in the wild. One unusually large flyer, a magnificent hummingbird, barely zooms over a woman's head as she reads an information panel. "Three grams! That's very light!" she says, as more hummers hover nearby.

Hummingbirds eat twice their body weight in food each day, a diet that consists of insects as well as nectar. Before migrating thousands of miles south for the winter, hummingbirds store a layer of fat equal to half their body weight! Including native plants in your yard can help hummingbirds survive such long journeys. Especially attracted to bright red flowers, hummingbirds sometime slow down at ocotillo and fairy duster plants long enough for you to see them eat or perch and clean their beaks. However, the hummingbirds remain mostly on the move, creating thrilling close encounters for humans in this habitat. "Hey girls, how about we sit and wait for them to come to us again!" suggests an enthusiastic mom. Within minutes, they are being buzzed again by some of the Desert Museum's most entertaining occupants.

Paleo Scene

Scan the horizon from a high point at the Desert Museum and you may barely notice the rock outcrops of the Mountain Woodland or Cat Canyon exhibits blending into the landscape below. Lush as any completely natural Sonoran Desert setting, the Museum grounds merge seamlessly into their surroundings. Sandy washes, or *arroyos*, snake in and out, winding by the dinosaur-age bulk of Brown Mountain. Views from the Geology Overlook stretch beyond fossil-bearing valleys into Mexico, more than 60 miles south.

Put on a pair of protective goggles and dig into the local past as you practice your fossil study, or *paleontology*, skills at Ancient Arizona. Grab a brush and a trowel, and experience what collector Richard Thompson must have felt in 1996 when he discovered the 100-million-year-old fossil of the dinosaur *Sonorasaurus* in the Whetstone Mountains east of Tucson. "I think I found one!" exclaims a young museum visitor, hoping to unearth an important find at the excavation site for kids. However, further digging reveals only more sand. "No. It's just dirt," he announces, continuing to search for replica bones and skulls anyway. An important element in paleontology, such determination is also necessary to build accurate educational exhibits. The Desert Museum has created an amazing replica of Thompson's dinosaur site that reveals exactly how the plant eater's bones were preserved in a wall of stone!

Crypto Scene

When you walk along the upper end of the Desert Loop Trail, you would never guess that this rugged mound of rubble was a human creation! This hollow hillside was formed by piling up a huge amount of earth, covering it with a skeleton of steel reinforcing rods, and then spraying on a coating of concrete. After the concrete hardened, the soil was removed through an opening at the end of building. Artificial rocks were placed on top along with real soil and living plants. Step into this work of "rock art" to discover what the main ingredients are for making habitats appear so natural at the Desert

Museum. See how the dome-shaped structure was built and how exhibit specialists fabricate realistic rocks that could fool a geologist from a distance!

Museum crews create big, small, whole, and partial artificial rocks using latex molds. First, repeated coats of the liquid rubber glop are brushed onto the rock and dried to capture fine details. More coats of latex rubber follow along with cheesecloth to strengthen the layers. After the flexible latex dries and a nonstick substance is applied, a "mother mold" is made from fiberglass, foam, or burlap that is saturated with resin, plaster, or cement. Next, the rigid mother mold is removed from the rock, followed by the rubbery latex form. Flipped over like a bowl, the two molds are reassembled, prepared with another nonstick layer, and filled with concrete, plaster, or plastic. Once the contents harden, the molds are removed and paint is applied to the new, replica rock. To fabricate a large overhang or cliff, permission is obtained from a landowner and plastic is placed on the natural formation for protection. Numerous molds are made and a jigsaw puzzle of replica rock is anchored to a steel framework built at the exhibit location.

Once you realize that many of the rocks are artificial at the Desert Museum, you may wonder why so few real rocks are used on the grounds. If authentic rocks had been excavated for use in exhibits, damage would have occurred to surrounding natural habitats. Since large equipment is necessary to move heavy, real boulders, lightweight replicas make exhibit construction easier. When crafted into ravines, cliffs, and overhangs, the imitation stone works to contain animals in realistic habitats that also conceal spaces for routine museum operations.

Wild Things

Brimming with hundreds of plants and animals, the Desert Museum introduces you to living organisms in settings so natural that everything seems wild. You can even learn how to find the most secretive animals when you purchase a "Tracking Animals" booklet at the museum entrance. Take this handy tool as you tour the different museum habitats and look for tracking stations along way. Each stop is equipped with an inkpad and a rubber stamp of an animal track that you can mark in your guide and take home to keep for future reference.

Tracking animals involves more than finding their footprints. Developing this skill requires real detective work such as locating scrapes, identifying feathers and bits of fur, or examining droppings called *scat*. Even if you do not see the animal, you may discover what it had for dinner or where it spent the night! Test out your tracking talents if you encounter a row of Xs crossing the Desert Loop Trail. You may have discovered signs of a bird that spends as much time on the ground as in the air. Roadrunners have two toes pointing forward and two backward, which can confuse beginning trackers. How do you know if this bird was coming or going? Search for other clues in the sand that may solve the mystery.

If you think all deserts are dry, barren, and dusty moonscapes, then the Sonoran Desert will surprise you. This 120,000-square-mile region is jam-packed with plants and animals living in a variety of habitats re-created at the Desert Museum, including mountain woodlands, grasslands, and streamside environments. Why is the Sonoran Desert so different than the sparse Mojave and Chihuahuan Deserts next door?

All deserts generally have high temperatures and receive low amounts of precipitation from rain or snow throughout the year. The amount of rain—and when it falls—makes this desert unusual. Pacific storms bring water to the region from December through March, while tropical monsoon rains from the Gulf of California zip in from July through September. Severe frosts and only one rainy season (during winter) occur in the colder Mojave and Chihuahuan Deserts, shortening the growing season in these areas. Here, more favorable conditions allow a wider variety of plants more time to grow, producing rich habitat for other living organisms. If you visit southern Arizona during the monsoon season, be prepared for some excitement and observe the weather with caution. Crackling lightning, booming thunder, and downpours create a natural spectacle throughout the Sonoran region nearly every afternoon.

Feathered volunteers and their human sidekicks often greet visitors to the Desert Museum. The barn owl's heart-shaped face appears ghostly white by night.

People have always been a part of the Sonoran region. Almost 2,000 years ago, the Hohokam people, who were farmers, built irrigation ditches to grow crops in the desert. They were followed by the Desert People, or Tohono O'odham, who lived on mountain-spring water in winter and grew crops using monsoon rainfall in summer. Today, most live nearby on the second largest reservation in the United States, where water is drawn from deep wells. Although their culture has modernized, the Desert People continue to practice an important traditional ceremony believed to bring rain to the region at a time that marks the beginning of the Tohono O'odham New Year.

The Desert Museum was proposed in 1951 by William Carr to educate people about the value of the Sonoran Desert. A conservationist with a passionate concern for the treatment of animals, Carr had inventive ideas for showing people how to become responsible for protecting the desert for the future. After the facility opened in 1952, Museum Director Carr took on the personality of "George L. Mountain Lion" in a series of newspaper articles to explain the natural history of the Sonoran Desert. Today, the mountain lion remains the captivating symbol of the Arizona-Sonora Desert Museum.

Otters, beavers, and eight species of native fish populate the museum's riparian corridor exhibit. Such streamside habitats provide wildlife with food and shelter in an otherwise dry region, but are quickly disappearing as a result of human use.

Travel Log

- Arizona-Sonora Desert Museum contact information: desertmuseum.org, 520-883-2702.
- To reach the Desert Museum from I-10, take the Speedway Boulevard exit (257) and travel west on narrow and twisting Gates Pass Road. Turn right on Kinney Road, and continue 2.5 miles to the entrance on your left. Oversize vehicles or cars with trailers should approach the Desert Museum from the Ajo Way exit off I-19. Travel west on Ajo Way (AZ 86) to Kinney Road, turn right, and continue 7.5 miles to the entrance.
- Facilities are open daily throughout the year. From October through February, hours are 8:30 a.m. to 5 p.m. From March through September, hours are 7:30 a.m. to 6 p.m. Admission is $9 for adults, and $2 for children ages 6 through 12. Younger kids are admitted free of charge. Memberships and group rates are also available.
- You will be outside most of the time during your visit, so be prepared for warm, sunny days by applying sunscreen and wearing a hat and comfortable shoes. Drinking fountains are conveniently located throughout the facility and opportunities to rest under shade ramadas arise frequently. Two restaurants are located at the Desert Museum along with a gallery and an excellent gift shop stocked with captivating reading material and souvenirs.
- While you are in the area, visit the Tucson Mountain District of Saguaro National Park (see page 116), which is located just a few miles up the road from the Desert Museum. Continue northwest on Kinney Road 7.5 miles to the Red Hills Visitor Center. Open daily throughout the year, Saguaro National Park protects dense populations of giant saguaro cacti, which grow only in the Sonoran Desert. Call the park at 520-733-5158 for further information.

Seven species of colorful, curious, native hummingbirds whir within inches of visitors in the hummingbird aviary, a highlight of the Desert Museum.

2 Chiricahua National Monument

Discovery Zone

Venturing up Bonita Canyon past curious figures cast in stone reveals an enchanting element of the Chiricahua Mountains that persists well beyond the end of the scenic road at Massai Point Nature Trail. Enjoy the roadside stops along the way and you will get wrapped up in anticipating the next interesting geologic feature around each bend. Visit an exhibit building constructed from welded volcanic tuff and enjoy a short walk on the nature trail to learn more about the native people and geology of the area. Then, take a moment to realize the momentous events—from volcanic explosions to Apache suppressions—that have occurred in this uncommon setting.

Rocks Around the Clock

Descend on foot from the rocky rim at Massai Point to an observation station along the Ed Riggs Trail for a bird's-eye view of all points west of the Chiricahuas. Use the feature finder (a simple viewing tube with major landmarks identified) to navigate your way around the region. On a clear day—and there are many of those—you can see Mica Mountain more than 75 miles away in Saguaro National Park! Willcox Playa bakes below in the sun while you are surrounded by countless pinnacles and mushroom rocks at a cool and comfortably high elevation.

Hiking is the best way to dive into this world of wild rocks. Some trails are more difficult than others, but each offers remarkable rewards. Views of Cochise Head and Sulphur Springs Valley cannot be beat from the Heart of Rocks Loop trail—provided you are able to hike the up-and-down 7.5 miles past Big Balanced Rock, Duck on a Rock, and Punch and Judy.

To experience a little bit of everything the monument has to offer, the Echo Canyon Loop is a terrific choice. Plan to trek counterclockwise on this 3.3-mile trail, so that the return trip is not an uphill endurance test. Pack a lightweight lunch and a camera because you will absolutely want to linger along the way. Every cool geologic formation in the park can be found along this route, from shingles and ribs to slot canyons and spherulites. Although the first 0.5 mile is steep and exposed, you soon begin to enter a weird volcanic world of sculpted stone and steep-walled canyons. On your way to Echo Park, look forward to entering Wall Street, a tall, narrow formation

Rhyolite pinnacles surround hikers along the Ed Riggs Trail, where views stretch 100 miles west beyond the Willcox Playa below.

of volcanic tuff not unlike a New York City skyscraper. Every hiker stops here in awe—and you will, too, when a strong breeze whistles through a slot in the rocks and you have to regain your balance to head on down the trail.

In the depths of Echo Park, water trickles along, nourishing a shadowy grove of the tallest Arizona cypress to be found. Stretching to impressive heights to capture elusive rays of sun, these monarchs offer hikers an opportunity to rest in the shade before hitting the sunny, south-facing side of the trail. Unique geologic deposits that look like hailstones can be seen along the way as you steadily climb back toward the trailhead. Noisy jays dart around through the pines as you reenter the forest, and before you know it, you have completed an exceptionally enjoyable trip into the heart of Chiricahua National Monument!

Paleo Scene

Find a high point along the Sugarloaf Trail or Massai Point Nature Trail to examine the rock-studded scenery of Chiricahua National Monument. Much of the land you see today originated near the blue-tinted mountains visible on the southern skyline—remnants of a volcanic basin formed 27 million years ago. Envision molten rock, steam, and hot gases trapped miles below the surface exploding into the air and bursting through layers of solid rock. Picture violent, repeated eruptions blowing scalding magma sky high into billowing clouds of red-hot gas, pumice, and ash over 1,200 square

Whimsical rock formations, including Cochise Head, a profile of the Apache chief rising from a ridge of volcanic tuff, appear throughout the Chiricahua Mountains.

miles of this landscape, ejecting more than a thousand times the amount of material that Mount St. Helens spewed in 1980! These events are not really so hard to imagine, once you have wondered what created the extraordinary rocks throughout Chiricahua.

After the ash settled and compressed, it turned into the rock now known as the Rhyolite Canyon Tuff, the 800-foot-thick bedrock of the monument. Later, cracks and joints in the tuff were eroded by water, plant roots, and organic acids, a process that continues today. Take a hike on any monument trail to encounter signs of ancient volcanoes or more recent erosion, where Ice Age freezing and thawing wedged huge blocks apart to form dramatic slot canyons and hidden grottoes. Along the way, you may notice fossil *fumaroles* (ancient steam vents), *solution pans* (dish-shaped depressions), and *chicken heads* (knobby protrusions). If you come across a deposit of *spherulites,* you may be fooled into checking for stormy weather—these marble-size balls of volcanic ash encased in crystalline minerals of quartz and feldspar look just like a pile of freshly fallen hailstones!

Crypto Scene

Identifying rock formations adds to the fun of any visit to Chiricahua, whether you are driving, hiking, or picnicking. One of the first sculptures you will see is the Organ Pipe, which towers above Bonita Canyon like a battalion of guards flanked by a forest of pines, firs, and oaks. Once a smooth block of volcanic tuff, repeated freezing, thawing, and weathering over the past 10,000 years split the cliff face into a group of cylindrical shapes that is more stable than it looks. Studies show that these columns could withstand 12 to 13 times their weight in stress before they budge. Even the 7.2-magnitude earthquake that shook southern Arizona in 1887 did not shift the pinnacles of Chiricahua.

As you explore the monument, watch for the one geologic personality that seems to keep an eye on everything for miles around. Cochise Head dominates the skyline to the north like a sleeping giant too ominous to disturb. Hike up the hill along the Massai Point Nature Trail to identify the facial features in the rocky ridge above. Named for the Chiricahua Apache chief, Cochise, this mass of volcanic rock bears a regal, curved nose and a prominent 8,109-foot forehead. Examine the profile more closely and you may even see the 100-foot Douglas fir tree that must be the biggest eyelash on earth!

Opportunities to hunt for other characters in the cliffs range from road-side pullouts along Bonita Canyon Drive to trailside vistas along the Heart of the Rocks Loop. Search for features such as Duck on a Rock or the Totem Pole to make the miles go by quickly on monument trails. Exercise your imagination, too. If you wandered around in this wonderland of rocksbefore it was mapped, what names would you have given to these whimsical geologic formations?

Wild Things

"Could that be a dog barking?" "I think I heard a turkey gobbling." Comments like these are often heard in Bonita Canyon at Chiricahua National Monument, where a rare migratory bird from south of the border can sometimes be seen. As you stroll along the trail toward Faraway Ranch, be alert for bright red and green feathers flickering through the streamside sycamores. Fluttering through the woods like a small flag of Mexico, the white-breasted *elegant trogon* makes a low, coarse sound that may not sound like a bird at all. If you hear such clatter, get your binoculars ready to see one of the most brilliant bird species in the Southwest.

International travelers from Mexico, elegant trogons migrate north in April and May to nest in particular areas of southern Arizona, especially where white-barked sycamore trees grow. Look for trogons in or near cavities up high in the sycamores from spring through about October. The round holes may be home to two or three young birds waiting for a tasty delivery of succulent insects from their parents. Cautious caregivers, adult trogons often become noisy to keep intruders away from their nests. Experienced birders from around the country come to Chiricahua, as well as the Cave Creek-South Fork area just east of the national monument, specifically to record the sighting of one of these "birds of paradise." Once temperatures cool off, the parrot-like trogons fly south as far as 500 miles to find warmer winter conditions in Mexico.

Micro Scape

Standing at nearly 7,000 feet along the Ed Riggs Trail, you can view an ocean of wild rock shapes surrounded by a low sea of sands and grasslands. Some refer to these mountains as a *sky island* of forested highlands isolated by the surrounding Chihuahuan and Sonoran Deserts below. Temperatures at the top of the Chiricahuas can be about 20 degrees cooler than the searing deserts below and precipitation can be twice as much as in the lowlands. This milder climate provides habitat for plants and animals that could not survive in the surrounding deserts. Although similar conditions exist in other Arizona sky island habitats such as the Huachuca and Santa Rita Mountains, many miles separate the ranges and the species that inhabit them. As a result, each isolated environment is unique.

When you explore the Chiricahuas, you experience a rich and unusual natural environment populated by a wide variety of plant and animals—some more common to Mexico than the United States. Located between a temperate climate to the north and subtropical conditions to the south, the Chiricahuas represent a biological and geographic crossroads. These mountains serve as the northernmost migration point for birds escaping the heat of Mexican summers, as well as the northern boundary beyond which

Birdwatchers from around the world flock to the Chiricahua Mountains for a glimpse of the parrot-like elegant trogon. Brightly colored red and green plumage makes this bird easy to spot when it emerges from the shelter of a streamside sycamore. Elegant trogons migrate north from Mexico in spring to secluded mountain canyons in southeastern Arizona. Most of the birds return to the warmer climate of Mexico in the fall.

photo courtesy of Jim Rorabaugh

many animals do not range and plants cannot grow. Species also vary greatly on north- and south-facing slopes, making Chiricahua National Monument even more intriguing with every step you take. Keep your camera and binoculars handy and be ready to catch a glimpse of a white-nosed coati or a collared peccary scurrying through canyons shaded by Mexican piñon pines and Arizona cypress. Just one such observation will make your visit to the monument that much more memorable.

Back in Time Line

If you had to rely on your hunting and gathering skills, could you survive in the Chiricahua Mountains? Abundant plants and animals—and precious water—here at Bonita Canyon, and in other locations such as Siphon Canyon in Fort Bowie National Historic Site to the north, made these mountains an ideal home for the Chiricahua Apaches. Agaves were roasted in large pit ovens and yuccas provided food as well as rope and soap. Acorns, walnuts, berries, piñon nuts, grapes, mesquite beans, and cactus fruit could be added to pronghorn, deer, or squirrel meat to create a complete menu. Shelters called *wickiups* were made by covering poles with beargrass and animal hides. Baskets woven from cottonwood or willow twigs and coated with pine pitch could be used to carry water from a stream. Yes, you could probably survive, unless you were kept away from your water source.

When pioneers, prospectors, and soldiers moved through this region in the mid-1800s, Apaches fiercely defended the most reliable source of water in the area—Apache Spring, now in nearby Fort Bowie National Historic Site. When a band of Apaches raided a local ranch in 1861 and Union Army troops were ambushed in 1862, people became edgy. Fort Bowie was then established to protect an important travel route and the source of water at Apache Spring. His band falsely accused of the raid and a kidnapping, Chiricahua Apache Chief Cochise waged a war on the U.S. military that lasted 10 years. Peace came for a while in 1872 and the Chiricahua Apaches were moved onto a reservation. Stripped of their freedom and basic necessities, the native people became discontent. After Cochise died of natural causes in 1874, the Apaches sought guidance from another Apache leader, Geronimo. After escaping to Mexico and enduring another 10 years of conflict, the Chiricahua people surrendered in 1886 and were shipped to Florida by railroad.

Visit the Erickson Cemetery just beyond the entrance to the monument and you will become acquainted with the first pioneers to settle here after the Apaches were removed. Raised on their farm and cattle ranch in Bonita Canyon, Erickson daughter Lillian started a guest ranch in the 1920s with her forest-ranger husband, Ed Riggs. Today, you can take a short hike up Bonita Creek to Faraway Ranch, which Lillian named because it was so "god-awful far away from everything." Despite its remoteness, Ed and Lillian treasured this rocky paradise and worked hard to help the area become a national monument in 1924.

Cemetery markers at Fort Bowie National Historic Site tell the story of life and death on the frontier. Fort Bowie was established in 1862 near a reliable source of water at Apache Pass between the Chiricahua and Dos Cabezas Mountains, where more than 20 years of battles were fought between settlers and Apaches.

Travel Log

- Chiricahua National Monument contact information: nps.gov/chir, 520-824-3560.

- To reach Chiricahua National Monument, travel east from Tucson on I-10 for 120 miles. Take the Willcox exit, and follow AZ 186 about 36 miles to the intersection of Bonita Canyon Road, and continue east to the monument entrance.

- The National Park Service offers daily tours of the main house at Faraway Ranch in Bonita Canyon, and an 8-mile drive takes you to overlooks at the Massai Point Nature Trail.

- Free shuttle rides carry hikers to Echo Canyon or Massai Point Trailheads. A 4.5-mile trek down Echo Canyon takes hikers back to the visitor center via the Rhyolite Canyon Trail.

- A first-come, first-serve campground is open year-round in Bonita Canyon. The monument is open daily from 8 a.m. to 5 p.m. Call 520-824-3560 for further information.

- If you are equipped with a high-clearance, four-wheel-drive vehicle, consider taking the Pinery Canyon Road to Portal to experience one of the most beautiful places in Arizona. When conditions permit, this dirt road takes you over the backbone of the Chiricahuas into stunning streamside woodlands occupied by rare birds such as the elegant trogon. Portal can also be reached from the east on AZ 80 at the New Mexico border. U.S. Forest Service camping is available in the area or check for lodging opportunities at the Southwestern Research Station by calling 520-558-2396.

- Plan on a fascinating side trip to Fort Bowie National Historic Site while you are in the Chiricahua Mountains area. From I-10 at Willcox, drive 22 miles south on AZ 186 to a graded dirt road leading to Apache Pass. In about 6 miles, you will reach a parking area, restrooms, and trailhead. Pack a lunch, water, and hike the 1.5 miles to the ruins of the 1894 frontier military fort. Along the way, you can read interesting trailside exhibits, visit the post cemetery, and investigate an Apache camp near Apache Spring, which features a fine example of a wickiup shelter. A visitor center includes restrooms, water, and a bookstore, and is open daily from 8 a.m. to 5 p.m. except Dec. 25. Call 520-847-2500 for details.

- For your rock collection: Rhyolite is a type of volcanic, or igneous rock, and is a good specimen to represent this area.

3

Grand Canyon National Park

"You'll know when you see one," a visitor tells a young birdwatcher as he approaches the observation area below Lookout Studio. "They are really, really big!" the man exclaims, stretching out his arms as wide as possible, which still is not wide enough for a condor. "There! Is that one?" asks the boy, reaching for his binoculars to scan the sky above Bright Angel Trail. "No, afraid not," replies the man whose camera and super-long lens appear prepared for an important shot. "Think of them as sort of a reverse turkey vulture, but much larger," he explains, as at least three vultures fly nearby. "The undersides of turkey vulture wings are black in the middle, where the condor wings are white."

By mid-afternoon, five or six huge, black condors perch on limestone ledges directly below Lookout Studio on the South Rim. Sunning, dozing, and watching people just as much as people are watching them, the condors may spend hours here, not far from hundreds of visitors. Occasionally, they launch themselves into the canyon, inspiring onlookers with their size and grace as they soar over the colorful chasm. Equipped with easily viewed identification tags on wings that extend to 9.5 feet, the raptors have become the most popular attraction at the Grand Canyon, where their numbers are increasing due to a successful reintroduction program started in 1996.

Another Side to the Story

Combine condor watching with hiking and camping on the North Rim for a one-of-a-kind, less-crowded Grand Canyon experience. Approach from the east over Navajo Bridge to get a good look at the Colorado River 500 feet below in Marble Canyon. Picture yourself crossing by ferryboat as miners, pioneers, and tourists did from 1872 until 1928, when the historic bridge was built. Take a side trip 4 miles upstream to Lees Ferry, where you can access the river and appreciate the isolation of Lonely Dell Ranch Historic Site. Ever since John Wesley Powell charted the Colorado River in 1861, Grand Canyon river runners have started their adventures here at river mile zero. Continue west toward the Kaibab Plateau along the colossal Vermilion Cliffs—condor country—where captive-raised birds are released into the wild.

The spectacular condor can be sighted from both the South Rim and the North Rim of Grand Canyon National Park, and these birds are often seen from observation areas near Lookout Studio.

Marked with identification tags and equipped with a transmitter so that it can be tracked by biologists, a free-flying condor soars over the Grand Canyon.

photo courtesy of Chris Parish, The Peregrine Fund

Thriving between 8,000 and 9,100 feet in elevation, expansive North Rim meadows and dense forests seem a world away from the drier South Rim at less than 7,000 feet. Practically paradise in summer, the North Rim features diverse habitats occupied by a variety of species that keep wildlife watchers on their toes. Looking for condors in this environment takes some practice, since these scavengers are seen feeding on the ground as often as they are viewed in the air. "I've seen turkey vultures and I've seen turkeys, but I haven't seen a condor yet," says a hiker along Widforss Trail. Wild turkeys can be spotted in small groups at the edge of forests and meadows where they eat seeds and fruit. Large, dark, and slow moving, they are sometimes mistaken for turkey vultures or condors from a distance.

"We saw 17 condors here at the same time," says a ranger at the Grand Canyon Lodge, where rambling patios cling to the rim, providing fantastic views of the buttes, temples, and pyramids below. Visitors equipped with cameras, binoculars, and a little patience are often rewarded here by the sight of an enormous bird gliding on the canyon currents. Even when the raptors are not present, the anticipation is fun as audiences gather around a massive limestone fireplace for the "Condor Talk" every afternoon. Plan to attend this presentation to learn more about condors and to increase your condor-watching success.

Set up camp nearby in the ponderosa pines of the North Rim Campground to enjoy crystal clear night skies and morning observations of silvery tassel-eared Kaibab squirrels. Known to live only on the North Rim of the Grand Canyon, these secretive animals leave behind gnawed twigs and piles of pinecone scales as signs of their presence. Humans sometimes leave things behind, too, so be sure to inspect your campsite before you depart. Ravens, rodents, deer, and even curious condors may pick up litter, which if eaten can lead to an animal's illness or death.

Whether you take a mule ride down the North Kaibab Trail, or just spend a day sightseeing from Point Imperial to Cape Royal, your chances of viewing an endangered species' success story are very good on the North Rim. "Did you see a condor come through here?" asks a visitor at Roosevelt Point along Cape Royal Road. "There it is!" calls out a young girl walking along the trail. Others gather with binoculars, ready to catch a glimpse of the park's most popular animal, just as one slow flap of its wings sends the bird sailing out of sight. "Well, I didn't see it, but that's the closest I've come yet," says another visitor, who like many, feel satisfied just knowing that condors have returned to the canyon.

Paleo Scene

Five or six million years may seem like a long time, but when you realize the rocks at the bottom of the Grand Canyon are billions of years old, millions seem like minutes! Erosion that shaped the canyon itself occurred only in the last five or six million years, as the Colorado River carved its way through uplifted layers of the Colorado Plateau, and rain, snow, and streams carried additional rock away. Some geologists suggest that the lower 2,000 feet of canyon was carved by the Colorado River only 750,000 years ago. Even today,

A sliver of 250-million-year-old Kaibab Limestone forms Angels Window along Cape Royal Trail on the North Rim.

Expansive panoramas from Cape Royal on the North Rim encompass a wealth of Grand Canyon geology and a variety of formations such as Wotans Throne.

the forces of erosion continue to work. Summer monsoon thunderstorms dump inches of rain, scouring canyon walls wider and deeper each season. Winter temperatures freeze water hidden in fissures, cracking rocks off into the canyon. Even the plants do their part as roots seek water and pry rocks apart.

Meet canyon geology close-up if you come prepared to hike down the Kaibab or Bright Angel Trails. Better yet, take your mind off the tough trek up by identifying rock layers along the way! Start by remembering how gneiss (nice) it is next to the river. Surrounded by dark *gneiss* and *schist* (warped, metamorphic rocks) almost two billion years old, you are ready to travel back up to modern times. You may miss a few million years here and there as you stop to catch your breath and enjoy views of the Colorado River, but in no time at all, you have passed the 520-million-year-old Tapeats Sandstone and conquered the greenish-grey Bright Angel Shale. Before you know it, Temple Butte Limestone gives way to the most spectacular crimson cliffs in the canyon—the 340-million-year-old Redwall Limestone, where most caves and arches form. Reds and tans of the Supai Formation give way to the rusty 270-million-year-old Hermit Shale next, as time begins to fly, and you enter the world of petrified dunes called the Coconino Sandstone. Yellows and greys of the 262-million-year-old Toroweap Formation announce one last layer to go—the whitewashed Kaibab Limestone, otherwise known as the "bathtub ring" of the canyon. Capping practically the entire canyon, this fossil-pocked 260-million-year-old formation marks the end of your journey through geologic history!

Crypto Scene

At least 1,000 caves have eroded out of the Grand Canyon's sedimentary rocks, creating safe hiding places for both animals and humans throughout time. Although park caves remain off-limits to visitors, researchers continue to study these hidden areas to protect the natural, cultural, and paleontological resources found within.

Cave exploration here in the 1930s revealed a variety of discoveries, from tons of *guano*, or bat droppings, to delicate figures made from willow twigs. Produced by an enormous colony of Mexican free-tailed bats, the guano was mined by prospectors for fertilizer. Although guano mining ended in 1962, the disturbance devastated roosting bat populations. In contrast, discoverers of the willow artifacts were more careful about their find. The three trail workers who recovered the "split-twig" figurines (made from a single twig twisted into the shape of deer or other game animal) delivered the artifacts to the South Rim museum. Estimated at 3,000 to 4,000 years old, the tiny relics revealed information about an ancient culture that inhabited the area known as the Desert Archaic people.

The most significant discovery of split-twig figurines occurred at Stanton's Cave in Marble Canyon, which was once habitat for the largest known maternity colony of western big-eared bats known in Arizona. A chain link fence installed in the 1970s at the cave entrance to protect artifacts obstructed the bat flyway. People continued to sneak into the cave, disturbing bats and archeological resources. Few bats remained until an iron, bat-navigable gate installed in 1996 worked to keep people out and allow the bats to move freely once again.

Cold, dry cave conditions preserve a wealth of valuable information, acting like storage facilities until scientists can inventory their contents. Even ancient condor nests and eggshells have been found preserved in canyon caves, proving the Grand Canyon was an important historical nesting area for the endangered birds. Bone fragments from fossil nests have revealed that condors once ate Ice Age mammoths, camels, and mountain goat species that are now extinct!

Wild Things

When young condor number 305 fledged from its South Rim nest in November 2003, the bird made history. Fully grown at only six months, it was the first wild-hatched condor to successfully fly from the nest since Arizona's recovery efforts started in 1996.

By the time this country was settled by Europeans, California condors—North America's largest flying birds—lived only in a narrow strip from Canada to Baja California, Mexico. Some returned in the 1700s when ranching introduced cattle, horses, and sheep to Arizona. Strict scavengers, condors

Big black-and-white adult condors are easy to spot with their 9.5-foot wingspan and bald orange heads. Immature condors have black-colored heads. Brought back from near extinction by a captive breeding program, condors released in the Grand Canyon area are now successfully raising young in the wild. Biologists monitor the progress of these federally protected birds, taking blood samples and inoculating them against dangerous diseases such as West Nile virus.

photo courtesy of Chris Parish, The Peregrine Fund

eat only large, dead mammals; many condors perished after consuming carcasses of predators that had been poisoned, such as coyotes. Egg collecting and museum collecting also reduced condor numbers in Arizona, until the last one was seen in 1924. Condors were included on the first Federal Endangered Species list in 1967. By 1982, only 22 remained in the wild—all in California. The only way to prevent extinction was to capture the last wild birds, breed them in captivity, and release their offspring into wild.

Tracking the Flight to Freedom

Captive breeding includes removing eggs as they are laid, which often causes adult condors to lay a second or third egg. The additional eggs are incubated, and chicks are raised by a person using a hand puppet that looks like a parent condor. This crafty technique prevents young condors from *imprinting* on, or developing an attachment to, humans. Chicks not raised by puppets are brought up by their own parent birds. Young condors raised this way have been released into the wild each year since 1996 at Vermilion Cliffs, just north of Grand Canyon National Park. Remoteness, caves, and plenty of food—deer, elk, bighorn sheep, and other animals—makes this a perfect place for condors.

Soaring up to 50 miles an hour and able to travel 150 miles a day, many of the released condors are content to live in the Grand Canyon. Females lay a single, 5-inch-long egg directly on the floor of a cave or on a rock ledge, and after 56 days, the egg hatches. Mating for life, the birds share the duties of feeding a young nestling by regurgitation. When young condor number

305 finally left the nest, its captive-raised parents continued their attentive care, along with biologists who monitor all the condors daily. Technicians track breeding and roosting activity, monitor movement, and study condor habitat using radio transmitters and Global Positioning System (GPS) devices attached to the bird's wings. Solar-powered GPS units transmit data hourly on a bird's precise location, and workers at the Peregrine Fund receive nightly e-mails with the GPS information.

Tracking is critical to locate condors and protect them from human encounters and environmental risks. Although the birds can live as long as 50 to 70 years, some condors have fallen victim to lead poisoning from spent ammunition in carcasses. Condors have also been killed by eagles, coyotes, or run-ins with power lines, and some have even been shot. Reliable tracking methods allow biologists to trap birds at six-month intervals to inoculate the condors for disease, test their blood for lead poisoning, and replace transmitters. Although seven years passed from the initial release of condors in Arizona to the first successful fledging of a condor in the wild, these scientific methods have increased expectations for reestablishing a wild population. In 2004, the entire population of wild and captive condors reached almost 250—from a low of 22 birds in 1982—with nearly 50 condors flying free over the colorful canyons of northern Arizona.

Micro Scape

"We've been reading *Brighty* on our way to the canyon," says a mom browsing through books at the North Rim Visitor Center. "It's fun to find the places that Brighty went with Uncle Jimmy Owens." Even though the classic tale of a friendly wild burro was first published in 1953, the illustrated book continues to stir imaginations of all ages. Readers always remember the stories of nature, wilderness, survival, and loyalty they learned from Brighty's trips up and down the canyon. Inspired by a real burro that lived on the North Rim of the canyon until 1922, the author included actual places and people in her writing.

> Especially on moonlit nights a shaggy little form can be seen flirting along the ledges, a thin swirl of dust rising behind him. Some say it is nothing but moonbeams caught up in a cloud. But the older guides swear it is trail dust out of the past, kicked up by Brighty himself, the roving spirit of the Grand Canyon—forever wild, forever free.
>
> Marguerite Henry, *Brighty of the Grand Canyon*

Hiking along the Uncle Jim Trail, or crossing Bright Angel Creek (the source of the burro's name), reminds readers of the animal's adventures with the government's colorful big-game hunter Owens. Anyone who has read the book will especially enjoy the lifelike bronze statue of Brighty in the sunroom of the Grand Canyon Lodge on the North Rim.

A small doorway leads into a natural cave above Harvey Meadow that once provided shelter for North Rim resident Uncle Jim Owens, a U.S. Forest Service game warden in the early 1900s.

Back in Time Line

Search for evidence of human history when you visit the North Rim, and you will discover everything from the remains of a 1,000-year-old pueblo to a pioneer camp built 100 years ago! Investigate the ruins at Walhalla Glades archeological site along Cape Royal Road to imagine how prehistoric people lived along the rim. Sturdy limestone slabs still mark the foundations of summer homes built by early residents who spent winters below in the bottom of the canyon.

Take the graded dirt road just south of the road to Point Imperial, and you will encounter a grassy, round meadow once grazed by livestock. Here at Harvey Meadow, "Uncle Jim" Owens established a camp to take tourists on trips across the canyon. Hired by the U.S. Forest Service in 1907 to shoot, trap, and remove predators to protect deer on the Kaibab Plateau, Owens killed hundreds of mountain lions. Deer overpopulated the area as a result, stripping the vegetation for food and dying from starvation. Conservation practices today acknowledge that a balance of predators and prey is important for a healthy ecosystem, and Harvey Meadow has returned to its natural condition. Look beyond the white-barked aspen trees and search the cliffs above for Jim Owens' shelter in the rocks. What other signs of earlier visitors do you see?

Travel Log

- Grand Canyon National Park contact information: nps.gov/grca, 928-638-7888.

- The Grand Canyon's South Rim can be reached by traveling 80 miles north of Flagstaff on US 180. To visit the North Rim, drive 105 miles north on US 89 and 55 miles west on US 89 Alt to Jacob Lake. Head about 45 miles south on AZ 67 to the North Rim.

- Visitor services on the North Rim are open from mid-May to mid-October. North Rim Campground campsites are available with reservations, but check at the campground for last-minute availability. The South Rim is open 24 hours a day, year-round. Admission fees are charged, and national park passes are accepted.

- Every North Rim excursion should begin or end with a visit to Jacob Lake Inn, where the cookies and milkshakes are known as the best in the West. Be prepared for some tough decisions, though. Old-fashioned shakes are prepared either thick or regular in a variety of flavors, such as mixed berry, mint, peach, or pineapple. Baked fresh every day, the creative assortment of cookies includes lemon sugar, chocolate parfait, cookie-in-a-cloud, peanut butter, oatmeal raisin, and others. Jacob Lake's unusually tasty cookies have admirers worldwide. Every year, the inn receives an order for two dozen lemon sugar cookies—from Hong Kong!

- For your rock collection: Several types of limestone, sandstone, and shale are among the many geologic layers exposed at the Grand Canyon, so it is tough to pick just one. It would be best to check a local rock shop or gift store to find your favorite. Or, perhaps you might consider a piece of gneiss or schist, two types of *metamorphic* rocks—rocks formed from older rocks, but changed by great heat and pressure—found in the Grand Canyon.

Every visit to Grand Canyon National Park's North Rim should include a stop at Jacob Lake Inn, where the menu reads like a kid's dream come true. Known far and wide for tasty cookies and old-fashioned milkshakes, the inn offers freshly made treats baked each morning.

South Rim visitors seem glued to the edge of an overlook as they take in the breathtaking panoramas of Grand Canyon National Park.

4

Hopi Mesas

Get ready for a different type of experience. A visit to the Hopi Mesas is a journey back in time more than 1,000 years. It requires that you sharpen your powers of observation and the ability to record the sights, sounds, and smells in your memory, since the Hopi request that no photographs, video recordings, sketching, or sound recordings be taken on the Hopi Mesas. "Visiting Hopi is a wonderful time to use your mind and heart to record what you are privileged to see," says the Hopi visitor newspaper called *Yee se'e, Welcome to Hopi.*

Hopi — Peaceful People

The Hopi Indian Reservation is a sovereign nation within the United States. Will you need a visa or a passport? No. However, you must bring a respect for the privacy of the Hopi people, their regulations, and their cultural traditions — especially their ceremonial dances. While in many ways the visual impressions gained within the reservation do not look appreciably different from other destinations in the Southwest, the visitor is actually an invited guest to a separate nation within the United States. Such a visit requires some preparation and understanding of a culture and a way of life that is not only very old, but also quite different from the general culture in the United States.

Have you tried piki bread? It is a traditional thin bread made from blue cornmeal and cooked on a hot oiled stone. Try an Indian taco, too. Both present the perfect opportunity to expand your cultural horizons. The Hopi are very friendly and eager to share part of their culture with visitors. As with many cultures, the Hopi will return the same courtesy and respect shown to them.

The history of the Hopi people in the region of north central Arizona reaches back more than 1,500 years. The agrarian lifestyle of the Hopi anchors their religion and the annual cycle of life. Ten of the 12 Hopi villages are on top of three mesas, which extend south from a larger land mass named the Black Mesa. The Spanish numbered the mesas, from east to west, starting with First Mesa, about 15 miles west of Keams Canyon. Each of the 12 Hopi villages, while all part of the Hopi Nation, has a separate government, comparable to the jurisdiction of a city government within a county

The Hopi villages blend into the mesa tops, reflecting a unity with the natural environment. As the visitor approaches each mesa, the detail of the village built of light-colored stone gradually emerges.

or state. It is important to understand the specific regulations and customs of each village.

Early Visitors

When non-Indians first started visiting the Hopi people during their religious dances, most people attended at the specific invitation of a Hopi tribal member. As a result, they often attended with an understanding of the religious purpose of the dance. As the number of people attending the ceremonies grew, the instances of uninformed visitors increased and so did the level of disrespectful behavior. The Hopi, too polite to confront visitors, often just closed the villages to outsiders in order to protect the sacredness of the ceremony. The Hopi people are, by nature, a generous people. Each village establishes it own rules about access and visitation, especially during these ceremonial activities. Make local inquiries before entering a village. Trading posts are often a good place to make inquiries, as are tribal headquarters. Villages that close during ceremonies are usually well marked, but it is better to confirm your status as a guest.

Specific guidelines are contained in the Travel Log section at the end of this chapter. Following etiquette in visiting the Hopi people or other tribes cannot be overemphasized.

The Hopi are renowned for their basket weaving, carved katsina dolls, pottery, and silver jewelry. While trading posts on the reservation, the cultural center, and museums are good locations to obtain a remembrance of your visit to the Hopi Nation, stopping in one of the numerous small shops or homes on the mesas is even more memorable. Look for signs directing you to the shop or home of a Hopi artist. Your experience often leads to establishing a personal connection and much greater insight about who the Hopi are and how they live.

Each mesa specializes in a specific craft. First Mesa produces katsina dolls, pottery, and weaving; Second Mesa, coiled baskets, silver overlay jewelry, and katsina dolls; Third Mesa, wicker baskets, silver overlay jewelry, textile weavings, and katsina dolls.

Much of the Hopi way of life is tied to agriculture, specifically the art of dryland farming of corn, beans, and squash. Planted in June, just prior to the arrival of the summer thunderstorms, corn seeds are planted in groups of five or six. The practice reflects the communal nature of the Hopi, who live in small groups to watch out and protect one another. Look carefully for the small fields of corn, often just below the mesas, in sandy slopes of washes, or at the mouths of canyons. As you view the cornfields, observe the periodic

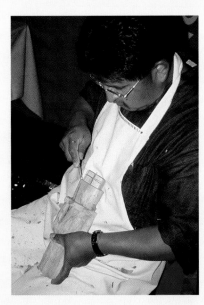

The true katsina doll is uniquely Hopi in its origin and is hand-carved from the root of a cottonwood tree. To ensure its authenticity, the collector should look carefully for the features and details that reflect the cultural traditions of the Hopi people.

photo courtesy of Jenny Michaels,
California Academy of Sciences

soil ridges. The ridges are intended to capture drifting snow and windblown rain to help nourish the seeds and the crop as it matures.

Hopi society is centered on the clan, or extended family. Rather than tracing family history through marriages, Hopi trace their ancestry only through their mother to their grandmother and so on, eventually leading back to the creation story of that clan. The name of the clan often reveals a part of that story, such as Water, Flute, Antelope, Bear, Mountain Sheep, to name a few. Clans include more than one family—for example, when a daughter marries, her new family will become part of her mother's clan, as will her daughters. The nature of the Hopi clan, consisting of many families, results in each Hopi having many, many relatives.

When a couple marries, the husband moves to the wife's village. He is expected to hold his wife's clan in highest respect, but continue to honor his own mother's clan. The clan is considered family and marriages within the clan are forbidden.

Clans control many aspects of Hopi life. The clan distributes the communally owned land to the families through the women of the clan. A daughter inherits property from the mother's clan. The women control the houses and furnishings. The men, responsible for things outside the village, manage the family herding and farming activities.

A certain amount of good-natured teasing occurs within and between clans. Humor is a frequent method for seeing just how far clan members will go to share their possessions and a gentle reminder of their special kinship. A key component of the clan system is the expectation that clan members must support and assist one another as necessary.

Micro Scape

Hopi are a deeply religious people. According to their religion, "The Hopi religion not only teaches peace and goodwill; Hopi people must also live it." Attending one of the ceremonial dances is a rare privilege. Dances are part of an active religion. Conducted for attainment, not entertainment, the ceremonial dances are part of a much broader way of life, the *lifeway* of the Hopi. Dancers seek to attain the good life of the Hopi. The Hopi lifeway includes a commitment to stewardship of the earth, respect and cooperation with others, and humility. Outsiders will never know or understand many of the highly personal and private significances of the ceremonies. Many central themes of value to the Hopi are respected by our culture, too.

Dancers, known as *Katsinam*, are sacred to the Hopi. Theirs is a most solemn responsibility. Ceremonies are held throughout the year, with the dates and locations determined by each village. In a manner of speaking, the Katsinam are messengers, collecting prayers or gifts from the people and carrying them back to the gods. Frequently the prayers are for rain, good health, and fertility.

Ceremonial Calendar

Three main ceremonies mark the Hopi calendar. A December winter solstice ceremony, recognizing and aiding the sun's return to its summer home begins the cycle. During this occasion, the principal Katsina opens the main underground kiva, or ceremonial chamber, in a village. This announces the return of the Katsinam. This ceremony can last more than a week.

It is followed by the arrival of the Katsinam in February. This ceremony helps the people prepare for the summer growing season. Bean seeds are germinated in containers and kept warm inside the kiva by fires kept burning around the clock to stimulate growth. Once the beans have germinated, they will be given away to village members during a dance ceremony. The February *Powamuya* ceremony is the time when youngsters between 6 and 10 are initiated into the Katsina Society.

The *Niman,* or "home dance," occurs after the summer solstice and celebrates the return of the Katsinam to their spiritual home in the San Francisco Peaks, north of Flagstaff. The dance, held in the village plaza, lasts one day and follows several days of ceremonies within the kiva. Dancers bring in the first stalks of corn that were planted in early June, demonstrating that the crops will be plentiful in the coming year. At the conclusion of the dance, the Katsinam solemnly file out of the plaza to return to their spiritual home. Social dances are interspersed among the three main ceremonies, celebrating the spiritual nature of various animals, rain, plants, and other aspects of the religious life of the Hopi. They are frequently held between August and February.

Foot races for boys and men, led by the Mudhead katsina, occur in April. These races symbolize the connection between the world that surrounds the Hopi and the spiritual world, since "as the men race, so the water will rush down the arroyos." The appearance of the Mudhead katsina anticipates the planting of crops. The Mudhead has a round headdress painted brownish red, usually with three gourds attached, one above each ear and the third on top of the head. It is sometimes called the Mudhead Clown katsina.

The gourd rattle with feathers attached, frequently used in ceremonial dances to maintain the rhythm of the dancers, can be painted or unpainted. Blue paint typically represents the sky and yellow signifies the sun.

The Hemis katsina is frequently chosen as the principal character during the Home or Niman Dance. Hemis wears a Douglas-fir neck ruff, a kilt, and a sash, with a fox pelt hanging from the belt in the rear, and carries a rattle and sprig of Douglas fir. The elaborate headdress, known as a tableta, is usually adorned with cloud and fertility symbols. Black corn soot covers the body of the dancer.

Katsina Dolls

Presented as gifts to infants, children, and adults during ceremonial dances, carved katsina dolls help children learn to recognize the various Katsinam. If you are fortunate enough to attend a katsina dance, purchasing a doll from a local artisan, Hopi cultural center, or trading post is an excellent remembrance of the privilege. Once you have witnessed a religious ceremony you will have a much better eye of what detail to look for in a carved katsina doll representing the dancers.

The carving of the katsina dolls has been a part of the Hopi tradition since the late 1800s. Katsina dolls carved by the Hopi people reflect an important part of their religion. Other tribes and even non-American Indian sources have attempted to reproduce the dolls, however most of them lack the accurate detail taught to the Hopi through their cultural traditions.

Back in Time Line

Visual comparison of the pueblos on the Hopi Mesa and the ancient dwellings of the Anasazi people of the Southwest are inescapable. The connection goes much deeper, however.

Settlement of the Hopi Mesas coincides with the establishment of other pueblos in the Southwest, including Wupatki (see Wupatki National Monument, p. 152), Betatakin (Navajo National Monument, p. 87), and dwellings

Hopi cornfields are small and carefully placed to take the most advantage of available moisture. Individual families tend them for their own use.

in Canyon de Chelly National Monument (see p. 86). Oraibi, on Third Mesa, established about A.D. 1100, is the oldest continuously occupied settlement in North America. Archeologists named the ancestral Pueblo culture the *Anasazi,* a Navajo word for the "ancient ones" or the "ancient enemies." The Hopi know their ancestors as the *Hisatsinom,* "people of long ago." The Hopi people are the descendants of the ancestral Pueblo people. One explanation for the abandonment of many prehistoric pueblos scattered across the Southwest is a gradual migration northward. Perhaps caused by a deepening drought, poor crops, or disease, the region witnessed gradual decline in the population. However, the northward migration is part of the Emergence Story of the Hopi, moving from the First World to the Fourth World. Divided into tribes after arriving in the Fourth or Upper World, the Hopi people set out on a series of migrations seeking a permanent home. Gathering from many ancient pueblos, the Hopi arrived at their present home on the mesas. They have stayed ever since.

Living in a Rock House

What is it like to live on top of a rock mesa? Do you feel a sense of ancient history as you walk the narrow streets lined with small houses? Many of the younger Hopi leave the reservation to obtain a college education, but many also return to the mesas. A deeply held sense of serenity is associated with growing up on the mesa tops. There is also a long history of family here and a close connection with the land. An important cultural distinction between most American lifestyles and that of the Hopi is their belief in the sacredness of the earth. Even their homes seem to spring from the mesa. Use of native rock as a construction material provides a greater sense of harmony with the environment and reduces the visual impact on the natural world.

Except for the occasional vehicle, power line, or satellite dish, the activities of the Hopi going about their daily lives on the mesas offer a glimpse of the vibrancy that once characterized the ancient abandoned pueblos scattered throughout the Southwest. Each of the villages determines the lifestyle that the people living there wish to live. The people of Oraibi have for many years resisted electricity and modern plumbing, preferring to maintain a more traditional lifestyle.

Touring the First Mesa village of Walpi provides visitors with a sense of time travel into the past. Walpi, the most authentic representation of the historic mesa-top villages, is the second oldest village and inhabitants work hard to maintain its historic integrity. A walking tour, offered for a small fee, takes about an hour and leaves the visitor with a much better appreciation for the Hopi people and life on a mesa.

Travel Log

- Hopi Mesas contact information: hopi.nsn.us, 928-734-3283.

- The Hopi Indian Reservation mesas lie along AZ 264, from Tuba City on the west to Keams Canyon on the east. Second Mesa is about 180 miles north of Flagstaff via US 89.

- It is a challenge to obtain information about the reservation prior to a visit, so you should plan on self-discovery as a significant element of your trip.

- The sites and destinations on the Hopi Indian Reservation are unique, sacred, and interesting. It is important to observe the following guidelines:

  - Wear appropriate clothing. Shorts, short skirts, and tightly fitted clothing are not acceptable. Wearing a hat to the Katsina Dances is not suggested.

  - Recording ceremonies with a camera, video camera, or audio recorder, or taking notes and making sketches are not allowed.

  - Check to ensure that no signs are posted closing the ceremony to outsiders. If unsure, check with local shops, village administration, or the village Community Development Offices.

  - Do not interrupt ceremonies. You are a guest observing a religious ceremony.

  - Alcohol and drugs are strictly prohibited on the Hopi Reservation.

  - Do not touch or remove any articles left as shrines or offerings. These objects may appear quite ordinary, but have much deeper significance to the individual who placed them and must not be disturbed. The same applies to archeological artifacts and sites, which are protected by federal laws and tribal regulations.

5

Hubbell Trading Post National Historic Site

"Now here's an eye-dazzler for you—and I don't just mean the rug this beautiful little girl is showing you," announces the auctioneer. Looking like a princess in her traditional Navajo dress and jewelry, the youngster slowly walks across the wooden stage to offer the audience a better view of the color-ful weaving for sale. Decked out in silver and velvet with moccasins and buckskin leggings, the girl appears shy in front of the crowd of bidders, but she charms the audience and the geometrically patterned rug sells for a good price in less than a minute.

Another traditionally dressed child, accompanied by her mother, emerges to show bidders a carefully woven Navajo wedding basket. Next comes a pair of youngsters displaying a Two Grey Hills–style rug. "Folks, this rug is natural, undyed, hand-spun, and hand-carded," explains the auctioneer. "Imagine how much time it took the weaver to make this one," he adds. A few bidders hoist their numbered paddles. Microphone in hand and dressed in a cowboy hat, jeans, and boots, the auctioneer zeroes in on a bidder who seems to want the rug. "Don't look at him when you're bidding," he jokes as the woman seeks agreement from her husband. To another person in the crowd he shouts, "Are you bidding or are you just stretching?"

Teasing the crowd makes for an entertaining performance enjoyed by both the young and old attending the Native American Art Auction at Hubbell Trading Post. Held twice a year under a huge, striped tent, this event draws artisans from throughout the Navajo Nation as they gather to sell handcrafted, one-of-a-kind items including weavings, carvings, jewelry, and baskets. Some Navajos attend to meet up with extended family members and others arrive to set up stands offering regional foods. Altogether, these activities produce a festive atmosphere where the public can participate in the legacy of the oldest traditionally operated trading post in the Navajo Nation.

Auction day is not only an ideal time to view an amazing assortment of Navajo crafts, it is also a good time to explore the historic site and learn about American Indian life directly from the Navajo people. You can take

Generations of travelers, traders, and Navajo artisans have passed through these rickety doors to the legendary Hubbell Trading Post. Commerce carries on inside much as it did back in 1876 when John Lorenzo Hubbell started his business.

Wearing a traditional dress and buckskin leggings, a young Navajo girl displays a colorful hand-woven rug for buyers at the Hubbell Trading Post Native American Art Auction. Purchases fund scholarships for Navajo students and contribute to preservation of the national historic site.

breaks from the auction to take a guided tour of the Hubbell home, chat with the post trader, visit the horse barn, or watch a weaver at work in the visitor center. Along your way, try a Navajo taco, a mouth-watering combination of beans, lettuce, tomatoes, and cheese piled high on a delicious circle of fresh fry bread. Listen carefully to your server, who may use the Navajo language while preparing your order. *Ahéhee* means "thank you" and *Hágoónee* means "good-bye."

A Slice of Life

When you open the rickety screen door to the trading post, you may feel that you are entering an old-fashioned country store. Wooden floorboards creak as you notice shelves stocked with staples such as cereal, peanut butter, and canned vegetables. Yet, unusual items such as thick loops of brightly colored yarn and bolts of velvet and satin cloth hint that this is not a typical grocery store. Through another doorway, the post trader speaks in Navajo to a young woman who is showing him a red-and-tan basket she has recently crafted. Nearby, visitors shop for dolls, necklaces, and postcards. Experienced

Brimming with baskets, blankets, pots, and colorful weavings, the Hubbell rug room contains hundreds of crafts made by skilled Navajo designers and by members of other Native American tribes.

collectors of Navajo weavings head straight for the rug room, an astounding space packed with stacks of blankets and rugs where Indian baskets hang alongside bridles and saddlebags that dangle from bulky ceiling beams. This is not just any corner market. This is a slice of real Navajo life where people buy, sell, and trade the same way they did when John Lorenzo Hubbell began his business here in 1876!

You can see how the Hubbell family lived in the late 1800s by taking a guided tour of the house located next to the trading post. Every surface of the interior is decorated with art, crafts, books, and furnishings collected by the Hubbells throughout decades of friendship and trading in the Southwest. Although it feels like a museum, this place was the Hubbell family home. Priceless rugs on the floor bear a history of footprints, including those of houseguest President Theodore Roosevelt. Famed artist Eldridge Burbank may have sketched the portraits on the bedroom wall, but these are the faces of Navajos and Ganado residents who were the Hubbells' extended family.

You will feel at home here, too, as a friendly farm cat accompanies you to the barn to visit the horses or over to the visitor center to see a woman weaving. Although an oversize loom is the centerpiece of the room, the visitor center also features books and other items for sale, including copies of metal trader tokens "good for $1 in merchandise."

Back in the shade of the auction tent, you can understand how easy it is to get caught up in the bidding, buying, and selling. Every item seems to have its own story. Another young presenter stands onstage showing the bidders a group of three very small weavings, colorful, but not very detailed. Bidding is slow and it is almost time to move to another item when the auctioneer speaks up. "Hey, everybody, these little rugs may not look like much now, but just wait until you get them home and put them on your table with a katsina or two." A few bidders raise their paddles and then the auctioneer adds, "By the way, these are practice rugs made by this 11-year-old beginning weaver, and she's looking forward to making some money on these so that she can buy pencils and paper when school starts in a couple of weeks." That steps up the pace and another minute of bidding puts a big smile on the girl's face as her little rugs sell for a good price on auction day.

Crypto Scene

Navajo legend lives on in each weaving you see at the trading post through the story of Spiderwoman. Believed to live atop 800-foot-high Spider Rock in nearby Canyon de Chelly, this supernatural being is said to have taught the Navajos' ancestors how to weave. The legend reveals that her husband made a weaving loom from sky and earth, and tools from white shell, sunrays, crystal, and lightning. Spiderwoman possessed a web ladder, which she used to descend from the towering rock. Elders told young children that if they misbehaved, Spiderwoman would carry them up the web ladder and consume them!

The legend includes the story of a young boy who was hunting in the canyon when he encountered an enemy and tried to hide. Exhausted, he found himself at Spider Rock, unable to escape. Aware of the legendary warning, he was startled to see a silken cord dangle from the rocky heights. He tied the magic cord around his waist and was able to climb Spider Rock. No hungry monster awaited him at the top. Instead, he found water, food, and his rescuer—Spiderwoman! She showed the boy how she made the strong web cord, anchored it to a rock, and suspended it to save him from his enemy. Once it was safe for the boy to leave, he thanked her and returned home to tell his tribe of Spiderwoman's great kindness.

Wild Things

Driving through the Navajo Indian Reservation on the way to Hubbell Trading Post, you may briefly encounter a meandering roadblock as a flock of sheep crosses the road. Easily herded from one grassy patch to another, most of the animals are ordinary balls of wooly fluff. Some certainly look wilder than others, though—especially the ones with four horns!

Spanish explorers brought *churra*, "coarse or scrubby," sheep to the Southwest 400 years ago. Pueblo Indians quickly realized the sheep's value for wool, flavorful meat, and dairy products and eventually taught the Navajo to spin, dye, and weave the strong, silky churro yarn. Herding and weaving soon became the Navajo way of life, but conflicts with settlers caused this lifestyle to come to a halt in 1864. The U.S. Army then forced more than 8,000 Navajo men, women, and children to abandon their huge flocks of sheep and march more than 300 miles in The Long Walk east to camps in New Mexico, where they were held in captivity. In the meantime, thousands of churros were slaughtered, stolen, or traded.

Navajos who survived the difficult conditions in New Mexico were allowed to return to their homeland in 1868. They received 14,000 churros and 1,000 goats from the federal government to build up new herds. Churro numbers increased into the hundreds of thousands, and concerns about overgrazing in the 1930s prompted the government to eliminate large numbers of the sheep until almost none remained. It is only through more than 30 years of hard work by the dedicated individuals of the Navajo Sheep Project that about 4,000 churro sheep survive today.

Older Navajos refer to churros as the "mother sheep" of the people. Some have no horns and animals with two horns are common. Four-horned rams are considered lucky because Navajo beliefs regard the number four as special. The long-haired churros come in a rainbow of earth tone colors accented by patterns that generate names such as *badgerface* or *pinto*. Churro yarn is now preferred by about 750 weavers who craft sturdy, smooth rugs and blankets with a special sheen produced only by churro sheep.

When you watch a weaver at work in the Hubbell Trading Post Visitor Center, you will catch an up-close glimpse of a colorful past being kept alive by a very skilled artisan. In the center of the room, a vertical, wooden loom supports an unfinished work of art as a Navajo woman slips a weaving fork into a maze of supple yarns. Brilliantly clothed in a traditional velvet blouse, colorful skirt, and turquoise jewelry, she is comfortably positioned on a stack of pillows next to some balls of black, brown, and white yarn. She nods OK to some people who ask to take her photo, but she rarely looks up, concentrating only on her detailed masterpiece.

Traders such as John Lorenzo Hubbell supported weavers by encouraging traditional techniques and providing examples of classic designs. Today, some weavers still raise and shear their own sheep, and wash, card, and spin the wool. They either use naturally colored wool or dye it using colors from native plants such as rabbitbrush, juniper, and walnuts. White yarn is used for the *warp*, the lengthwise set of cords used to string the loom. Yarn that crosses and interlaces the lengthwise threads fills in the fabric of the rug and is called the *weft*.

Observe the care used by the weaver to pack down the weave with the fork and consider how this repeated action results in such a well-planned design. The result may be a rug identified by its color, such as Ganado Red or

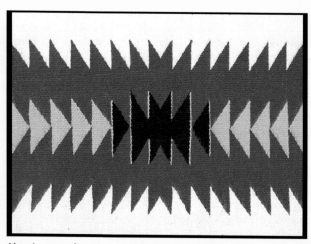

Many Navajo rug styles are named for towns within the Navajo Nation. With a classic design, Ganado rugs often feature a red background, dark border, and geometric shapes in black, white, or gray.

Two Grey Hills, or a creative pictorial style featuring cowboys, horses, and pickup trucks! Back at the rug room in the trading post, you will see even more styles: Burntwater, Chief, Wide Ruins, Storm, and Tree of Life. Once you learn to "read" Navajo weavings, your travels on the Navajo Reservation will be even more interesting. Every place on the map and each view from your window will remind you of a woolen work of art.

Back in Time Line

Look north across the wash from the trading post and you will see Hubbell Hill, the final resting place of one of the most well-known Navajo traders who ever lived. Although his grave site is not designated (according to Navajo tradition), John Lorenzo Hubbell left a lasting mark in many ways—as a merchant, translator, politician, and friend.

Born in 1853 in New Mexico, Hubbell was a self-educated man who became interested in the Navajos while traveling in the Southwest as a clerk and Spanish interpreter for the U.S. military. He began trading around Ganado in the early 1870s and built the present trading post in 1883. Navajo people enjoyed gathering at the post and often sought Hubbell's assistance in writing letters, understanding government policy, and caring for their sick. Lorenzo and his wife, Lina Rubi, even used their own home as a hospital when a smallpox epidemic occurred in 1886.

The Art of Business

Hubbell Trading Post was—and still is—a hub of life on the Navajo Reservation, as you can see by the hustle and bustle of business going on in the building every day. In fact, the sounds you hear today, boots clomping across the wooden floor and soft-spoken requests for canned goods off a shelf, have not really changed throughout the past century. The purpose of the post has always been to provide the Navajo people with food and merchandise while encouraging the appreciation of Navajo arts and crafts far beyond the Navajo Nation. Hubbell influenced weavers by showing them which traditional designs were popular with buyers. He even took apart old blankets to explain how a pattern was created. Hubbell also promoted the art of silversmithing, introducing the Navajos to Mexican silverworking methods.

Hubbell's successful business endeavors included farming, mail delivery, a blacksmith shop, livery service, and a wagon freighting business that operated out of his sandstone block barn, the largest in the region. Goods shipped out of Ganado included piñon nuts, corn, and thousands of pounds of raw wool provided by the Navajos to be sold in Gallup, New Mexico. Throughout the years, the Hubbell family established a merchandising network of more than 30 trading posts, two wholesale stores, curio shops in Hollywood and Long Beach, California, and a series of mail order catalogs. By the time Hubbell died in 1930, he had created solid social and economic relationships that crossed both cultural and geographic boundaries.

Some trading practices have changed with modern times, but traditional traders are still found throughout the Navajo Nation. Traders must know how to buy, sell, and trade for jewelry, pottery, baskets, weavings, and other crafts from tribes throughout the Southwest. An operator of a modern trading post nearby explains that a good trader has to be a people person. "Kids bring in their report cards and I give 'em a dollar for every A," he says. The generous merchant was rewarded for being a good trader when he encountered one of those kids at a local college. "The girl's getting her master's degree and she said, he 'used to give me a dollar for every A!'"

Travel Log

- Hubbell Trading Post National Historic Site contact information: nps.gov/hutr, 928-755-3475.

- Hubbell Trading Post National Historic Site is located on the Navajo Indian Reservation, 1 mile west of Ganado, Arizona, on AZ 264. Visitors traveling on I-40 can take US 191 north for 35 miles to Ganado. From Gallup, New Mexico, take US 491 (formerly US 666) north to AZ 264, then go west. The site is 53 miles northwest of Gallup, 190 miles west of Albuquerque, and 156 miles east of Flagstaff.

- The National Park Service site is open daily from 8 a.m. to 5 p.m. (6 p.m. in summer) except Jan. 1, Thanksgiving Day, and Dec. 25. Call 928-755-3475 to inquire about specific auction dates.

Morning mists unveil a rainbow over Hubbell Hill, across the dry wash from the trading post. When John Lorenzo Hubbell died in 1930, he was buried high on this knoll overlooking his home and business. The grave remains unmarked, according to Navajo custom.

6

Kartchner Caverns State Park

Discovery Zone

Think about what you would do if you had discovered Kartchner Caverns. Would you want to tell your family about the breathtaking underground formations you had seen? Could you postpone sharing your find with friends or teachers? What if you had to keep your good fortune a secret, not just for a while, but for many years?

Explore Inner Space

Answers to these questions await you around every corner when you are joined by a guide to explore the glistening recesses of Kartchner Caverns. Pass by the original entrance used by cave explorers in 1974 and you will see a ladder positioned at a sinkhole leading into the limestone labyrinth. Inching along through openings the size of coat hangers and crawling hundreds of feet in muddy darkness, Gary Tenen and Randy Tufts discovered a pristine cave undisturbed by human footprints. "We don't have to do that today," jokes the park ranger. "Anyone disappointed?"

A quick lesson in cave ethics makes some important points before you enter the massive steel doorway that looks more like a bank vault than a cave entrance. Although cameras, chewing gum, and sunglasses are left behind, everyone still carries lint and bacteria on their bodies that could harm the cave ecosystem. All agree to touch only the handrails inside, so that nothing is broken and no oils or microorganisms are transferred to cave formations. A brief walk through an airlock equipped with gentle misters ensures that microscopic debris from the outside world remains primarily on the visitors.

At Kartchner Caverns, you can compare how fresh the formations appear compared to those in other caves you may have visited. Conservation chambers work like buffer zones, keeping dry, desert air outside and warm, tropical air inside. This cave still "breathes" through the sinkhole, replenishing oxygen to the underground environment, yet the 99 percent humidity is maintained, which keeps formations growing. This series of protective design features works to build curiosity by the time the last steel door is reached before entering the cave. Identifying a couple of youngsters in the group to help as tour guides, the park ranger asks for some assistance. "Push that green button," he says. As the enormous door opens, he exclaims, "Let's go caving!"

At almost 60 feet, this towering central column called Kubla Khan awes visitors in the Throne Room of Kartchner Caverns. Photo courtesy of Arizona State Parks

Amber lights focus on a beautifully decorated world of cave formations, or *speleothems*, that quickly become fun and challenging to identify. Specially designed to emit a wavelength unsuitable for growth of algae and bacteria, the lighting seems to magically turn off as each tour group passes, returning the cave to its natural darkness. From every surface of the cave ceiling, *stalactites* hang down like ancient icicles. Their counterparts below, *stalagmites,* guard practically every bit of ground. Useful tips are offered by the ranger along the way. "Just remember 'c' for ceiling in stalactite and 'g' for ground in stalagmite."

Different minerals color an array of wildly shaped formations, some of which are named for foods such as butterscotch, strawberry cheesecake, or fried eggs. The park ranger assigns a young caver the task of carefully shining a flashlight behind a wavy crimson shape. "If this is bacon, it's very lean," he says. "Red is from iron and purple comes from manganese," he adds. Everyone becomes a student of this calcite classroom as they learn to identify squiggly *helictites,* elegant *draperies,* and *columns.* "Shields develop from water seeping under pressure, like holding your thumb over the end of a garden hose," explains the guide.

Winding around through the moist cavern, visitors sometimes receive "cave kisses" of water droplets falling on their heads. "If moisture is the life-blood, then mud is the heart," explains the guide as an ocean of mudflats comes into view. Hanging from a low alcove, hundreds of delicate soda straws seem ready to fall under their own weight, as those sticking up from the thick muck did thousands of years ago. In some places, the slog measures 20 feet deep, like a giant sponge reserving water for the cave to drink up when it gets thirsty. Also visible is a section of the cave discoverers' original trail, which appears here and there throughout the caverns. Cave resource crews use only this established route to keep further disturbance to a minimum.

Once you marvel at one of the world's longest soda straws and become comfortable within the wet, living, layers of flowstone, this subterranean wonder feels almost familiar. "It's time for an open-cave test!" announces the guide. He shines a flashlight at individual formations and the group identifies each without error before answering a final question: "What are some things we experience here, but not in daily life?" "Quiet," replies the group in unison. After a few moments to sit and enjoy the cave in silence, everyone agrees with the guide. "Amazing that something so simple as water could create such magic!"

Paleo Scene

Blocks of limestone buckled up in the steeply tilted Whetstone Mountains contain compacted layers of the mineral calcite, formed millions of years ago from dead marine animals. Hundreds of thousands of years ago, rainwater carrying carbon dioxide (mostly from the soil) started seeping through cracks in the limestone, dissolving channels in the rock. As groundwater drained

Paleontologists have uncovered lots of evidence of prehistoric life in Kartchner Caverns. This Discovery Center exhibit recreates an 86,000-year-old Shasta ground sloth whose remains were found hidden in a labyrinth of the underground environment.

Like aging curtains suspended in a time-forgotten castle, drapery formations decorate many walls throughout Kartchner Caverns. These formations are created when surface water slowly dissolves limestone and deposits layers of calcite over thousands of years.

photo courtesy of Arizona State Parks

A young visitor marvels at a display featuring muddy boots worn by the original explorers of the cave. The Discovery Center includes interactive exhibits, a theater, and a gift shop that sells bat puppets.

away, openings in the Escabrosa Limestone dissolved further, creating huge chambers filled with air. Formations started to develop about 200,000 years ago, the same way they continue to grow today.

Rainwater dissolves calcium carbonate in the limestone. Once this solution reaches the cave, it releases trapped carbon dioxide the way soda "pops" when you open a can. Each drop leaves behind calcite and other dissolved minerals, which start creating *speleothems,* or cave formations. Look for water droplets falling from a stalactite on the ceiling of Kartchner Caverns. Splashing on the cave floor, the drops leave more minerals behind to produce a stalagmite. How much time do you think is necessary for the two formations to meet and create a column? Scientists estimate that 1 inch of growth requires 750 years!

Different shapes result, depending on whether the water drips, seeps, pools, condenses, or flows. Delicate soda straws grow longer as water runs through the hollow tube of a stalactite and deposits calcite at its tip. Slowly seeping water spreads out into shields, helictites, and cave cotton. Your journey into the caverns will reveal cave pearls crafted from pooling water, corraloids from condensation, and canopies created from flowing water.

Crypto Scene

Visit the Discovery Center to learn how cave bats roosting in the Big Room maintain an important connection between the outside and underground environment. After munching their evening meals, the bats excrete waste, or *guano,* a main link in the cave food chain. Large piles of guano accumulate and provide nutrients for most other living organisms in the cave ecosystem. First to the guano lunch lineup are bacteria and fungi, which are dined on by lice, mites, nematodes, and other hungry invertebrates. Scorpions, spiders, centipedes, and millipedes make a meal out of them next, as beetles and crickets move in last for dessert.

Most animals found in caves are *troglobites,* or cave dwellers, which can only survive in total underground darkness. Since they do not need to see, they are usually blind. Such permanent cave residents remain white or colorless because they do not need pigmentation to protect them from the sun. *Troglophiles,* or cave lovers, such as cave crickets, can live their entire lives inside the cave, but can also survive aboveground. Bats are cave guests, or *trogloxenes,* that live part of their life cycle in the cave, but must travel outside for food. Without trips to the surface by the bat colony—which eats about a half-ton of insects each summer—there would be no guano to feed other cave organisms. When scientists studied Kartchner bat populations from 1988 to 1991, only the Big Room contained fresh guano. Further analysis showed that two large piles of old guano in the Throne Room, and some smaller piles of guano in the Rotunda Room, were 40,000 to 50,000 old!

Wild Things

Consider yourself merely a visitor when you tour the Big Room, because this cave actually belongs to a bunch of bats! Conditions in the Big Room provide an ideal summer home for between 1,000 and 2,000 insect-eating cave bats that annually nest and raise their young at Kartchner Caverns. Pregnant females arrive at the colony each April, and each gives birth to one pup by late June. Babies stay in the warm roost while their mothers venture into the desert after sunset to hunt for mosquitoes, termites, flying ants, and other insects—serving as a natural pest patrol for local communities! By mid-August, young bats take test flights outside the nursery, and by mid-September, the entire colony begins migrating south to a winter hibernation roost in Mexico.

When biologists studied the Kartchner bats to understand how development of the cave might affect roosting colonies, they confirmed that summer was an especially important time to protect the bats. Between late May and early July 1991, the number of bats exiting the cave declined mysteriously. After 45 bat carcasses were discovered, observers witnessed a ringtail exiting the cave and later saw the raccoon-like raider guarding the cave exit. Bats eventually began using the cave again, despite the possible presence of a predator. The ringtail moved on, but the incident showed that disturbance during maternity significantly affects bat behavior. In addition, it proves

Visitors ride an electric tram through the desert that surrounds the Discovery Center to the dripping darkness beyond the entrance to Kartchner Caverns.

photo courtesy of Arizona State Parks

the superiority of Kartchner Caverns as a roost—bats like it so much here, they are willing to risk being eaten by a predatory ringtail to fly in and out of the cave.

Minimizing disturbance to the bat colony—especially while pregnant females and young live in the cave—is a priority at the state park. Limiting public tours in the Big Room to mid-October through mid-April helps cave bats survive and keeps Kartchner Caverns a dynamic underground ecosystem.

Micro Scape

Preserving the cave's natural environment comes first at Kartchner Caverns. From the early stages of development, biologists, geologists, hydrologists (scientists who study water), and other scientists studied the cave and recommended sensitive construction techniques and methods for monitoring environmental changes.

Temperature, humidity, and carbon dioxide levels throughout the cave are tracked by a series of monitoring stations maintained by a cave resource crew. Crew members also monitor human impacts and are responsible for routinely hosing cave pathways to remove hair, lint, and other particles that accumulate each day. Pumps drain off the water, which is recycled to irrigate landscaping near the Discovery Center building. When you board the tram to the cave entrance, you discover that water quality in and around the cave is particularly important. Designed so that no contamination occurs from gas-powered vehicles, the electric tram over Guidani Wash offers your first opportunity to participate in protecting the natural environment at Kartchner Caverns.

Back in Time Line

When you visit Kartchner Caverns, you sense a rare story of stewardship that started with cave discoverers Randy Tufts and Gary Tenen. Discouraged by litter and vandalism found in many discovered caves, Tufts wanted to locate an unknown cave. Following a tip in 1966, he located a sinkhole leading to a small room in the limestone. Busy with college in Tucson, Tufts could not continue his exploration until 1974, when he returned with his friend Gary Tenen. Inside the limestone space, a telltale breeze and the smell of bat guano hinted at larger chambers beyond. Squeezing through a tight blowhole, the cavers were eventually able to stand and walk for hundreds of feet, assisted by the glow of their headlamps. In the limited light, they were astounded by untouched surroundings decorated by sparkling soda straws and twisted helictites.

Careful to minimize their presence, Tufts and Tenen worked to preserve the cave on future explorations by staying on their established trail and keeping other areas off-limits. In some sensitive areas, they continued in socks, rather than leave footprints. Since word travels fast in the caving community and the location was near major highways, they decided to keep their discovery secret. "It was a caver's dream," according to Tenen, and the two worked tirelessly to protect it from destruction.

"It depended on us to take care of it," said Tufts. The cavers knew that so many people would want to enjoy the cave, the best way to preserve it would be as a public park. Working with the Kartchner family, who owned the land, and the State of Arizona, the two made sure a bill was passed in 1988 before others could find the cave. Fourteen years of secrecy had gone by, protecting the underground sensation until experts could participate in plans to develop Kartchner Caverns State Park.

Travel Log

- Kartchner Caverns State Park contact information: desertusa.com/azkartchner, 520-586-4100.

- Kartchner Caverns State Park is located 50 miles east of Tucson. Take the Sierra Vista exit (302) from I-10, and travel 9 miles south on AZ 90 to the park entrance at the base of the Whetstone Mountains.

- Exhibits in the Discovery Center captivate every visitor's imagination and provide information about the cave environment that is most appreciated after the cave tour. The theater features a video about the discovery of the cave and delivers an outstanding stewardship message. Camping, hiking, and picnicking are available, so plan on a variety of activities in addition to your cave tour.

- Outside temperatures average in the mid-90s during summer and the 60s during winter. Temperatures inside the cave remain a constant 68 to 69 degrees, but the humidity is always 99 percent, so believe the park rangers when they say you do not need a jacket inside the cave!

- Photography is not permitted in the cave so that everyone can enjoy the natural soundscape and subdued lighting.

- Kartchner Caverns is open 7:30 a.m. to 6 p.m. daily, except Dec. 25. Arizona State Parks recommends advance reservations by calling 520-586-CAVE (520-586-2283).

- Tour prices vary according to age. Rotunda/Throne Room Tours are offered year-round (children under 6 admitted free). Big Room Tours are offered only from Oct. 15 through April 15 to protect nesting bat colonies (no children under 6). A park entrance fee is free with a cave tour reservation. For general information, call 520-586-4100.

- For your rock collection: Limestone is the key rock formation at this destination; try rock shopping in the nearby town of Benson.

7

Kitt Peak National Observatory

Borrowing from the familiar warning on the rearview mirror on automobiles, a sticker on the side of a telescope at Kitt Peak National Observatory warns, "Objects in the mirror are further than they appear." The humor reflects the unusual nature of the work of astronomers and helps them keep time and distances in perspective. Light collected by the telescopes often started its journey toward earth hundreds, thousands, even millions of years ago. So astronomers are looking back in time and through great distances.

Have you ever tried to count all the stars in the night sky? If you started counting all the stars at a rate of one every second, it would take you 15,000 years to count all of them. Astronomy deals with very large numbers and very great distances. Astronomy has an inherent "wow" factor, much like the science of paleontology.

Stargazing allows you to have an armchair adventure. Stargazing also presents a chance to time travel. Star light is ancient light. To help us understand the great distances involved, imagine a penny represents our solar system; the next closest star is Alpha Centuri and it would be 200 feet away from the penny. Light, which travels through space at 186,000 miles per second, takes 13 hours to cross our solar system. At this speed, the light from Alpha Centuri takes four years to reach earth.

Kitt Peak has the distinction of hosting more optical telescopes than any place in the world. In addition to the 22 optical telescopes, Kitt Peak has two radio telescopes. The fact that this is very much a working observatory for the exploration of deep space affords opportunities for visitors that many other observatories do not offer. If you are interested in learning to navigate the night sky and view objects through one of two telescopes dedicated for participants, you will not be disappointed. Programs at Kitt Peak are unlike any others offered in the United States. Combining these special programs with the fact that Tucson hosts one of the largest amateur astronomy clubs in the country, it is of little surprise that this is a destination for people from around the world.

Save a visit to Kitt Peak National Observatory for summer to enjoy both the night sky and a break from the heat. Losing about 3 degrees for every

The Mayall 4-meter telescope dominates the Kitt Peak skyline, with the smaller 2.3-meter telescope to the left.

The Very Long Baseline Array (VLBA) antenna on Kitt Peak is one of 10 antennas collecting radio waves from distant stars. The combined power of the antennas collects detailed information on such exotic objects as quasars.

1,000 feet you gain in elevation makes this dramatic mountain summit 15 to 20 degrees cooler than lower elevations in Phoenix and Tucson.

Reaching for the Stars

Did you ever stare at the night sky and wish you might be able to get a closer look at the specks of light to see more detail? The curiosity of many people led to the development of the observatories that dot the summit of Kitt Peak today. One of the most unusual aspects of this collection of portals into space is the fact that Kitt Peak is an active research facility. That distinction presents visitors with both a challenge and an unusual opportunity.

Can you explore the sky during daylight hours? Actually, you can. Start with the visitor center, take a tour of the Mayall four-meter telescope, and visit the McMath Pierce solar telescope. With many of the scientists asleep in the various dormitories on the observatory grounds, you may conclude that not much is going on. As you might expect, however, the real story happens at night when the adventure of witnessing the birth and death of galaxies and stars presents itself to the explorer.

The mountain awakes as dusk approaches, and like the eye of a sleeping giant, the opening of the dome on the four-meter telescope signals the other astronomers that evening conditions are suitable for deep-space viewing. One by one, the doors on the domes open, and each astronomer begins his or her evening's work. With recent technology advances, astronomers may guide the instruments by computer links from thousands of miles away. The remote control of the telescopes lends an eerie element to the movement of the telescope domes, rotating to follow an object in the sky without anyone in sight.

The staff at Kitt Peak offers a Nightly Observing Program, with the chance to use a 16-inch or 20-inch state-of-the-art telescope and learn about the formation of our universe. An evening program is an enriching experience that will help you navigate the night sky on your own. Watching the sunset begins the Nightly Observing Program, getting you in the mood to view the night sky. As darkness increases, the night sky begins to reveal itself, with the brightest objects setting the framework and the faint deep space objects slowly coming into to view. The program, which lasts three or four hours and includes a box lunch, leaves participants with much greater confidence in navigating the stars on their own.

If you want to alter your circadian rhythm and get in harmony with the astronomers, an Advanced Observing Program allows the amateur astronomer to spend the night on Kitt Peak and use the telescope to explore the night sky. The program allows for a visual survey of the universe and the opportunity to take photographs of objects through the telescope to carry back as mementos of your tour of the universe.

Both the Nightly Observing Program and the Advanced Observing Program require reservations.

Crypto Scene

Have you ever listened to the stars? Does that sound strange? Stars not only send light waves toward earth, but our planet also receives invisible energy at different wavelengths and frequencies. In the early 1930s, radio engineer Karl G. Jansky discovered radio waves were coming from the Milky Way. Several years after the initial discovery, a second radio engineer built a radio telescope designed to collect and concentrate these faint radio frequency (RF) waves. Since the signal strength is relatively weak, the RF energy was collected with large parabolic collectors and then amplified through a radio receiver. This was the first radio telescope.

Scientists reasoned that two or more radio telescopes could be linked or arrayed together to gather radio frequency waves at the same time. If the radio waves collected by multiple telescopes are precisely synchronized (radio interferometry) by computer, each radio telescope dish becomes just one part of a very large telescope. The result is equivalent to a single antenna that is 5,000 miles across. This system of radio telescopes is called a Very Large Baseline Array (VLBA). One of the 10 VLBA antennas is located on Kitt Peak; of the remaining nine, eight are located in the United States and one is located in St. Croix, Virgin Islands.

As the idea became more refined, the technique provided new images and much more detailed information than ever before on the birth of the solar system, the information arriving in the form of electromagnetic energy outside the visible spectrum of light.

Radio waves collected through each of the 10 antennas reveals details about deep-space objects, such as stars, galaxies, black holes, and quasars, presenting the information in a single image. The digitized data from the antennas are combined into one image at Socorro, New Mexico.

Socorro is also near the home for the Very Large Array (VLA), a separate collection of 27 large movable antennas mounted on railroad tracks, which function in much the same united way as the VLBA. The radio wave images from both the VLBA and the VLA allow astronomers to very accurately record and measure the motion of subatomic particles and gases on the surface of stars, recording the birth and explosive death of stars over 10 million light years away from earth. The VLA was the backdrop in scenes from the motion picture *Contact*.

Micro Scape

Kitt Peak and the surrounding landscape is part of the Tohono O'odham Indian Reservation. As the second largest Indian reservation in the United States, it is almost as large as the state of Connecticut. Spanish explorers called the Tohono O'odham, *Papago*, meaning "bean eaters." The Papago changed their name to Tohono O'odham or "desert people." The name is much more reflective of their heritage and traditions.

Possible descendants of the prehistoric Hohokam, the Tohono O'odham lived in the area now known as Phoenix and Tucson. Still visible in parts of the valley, the advanced network of irrigation canals built by the prehistoric Hohokam reflects the scientific ingenuity of a much earlier culture. Their technological advances preceded the exploration of stars, but were just as advanced during their time as the construction of a giant telescope is for our time.

From the summit of Kitt Peak, you can see Baboquivari Peak to the southwest. Rising dramatically to 7,730 feet, it is the home of I'itoi, Elder Brother to the Tohono O'odham people and a key figure in their creation story. According to their legend, when First Born finished preparing the earth for his people, the first inhabitant was I'itoi, followed by Coyote and Buzzard. I'itoi created people from the clay of the earth. He also created the "crimson evening," the light of sunset that bathes the mountains of the reservation in radiance as darkness falls. I'itoi is the spirit of goodness for the Tohono O'odham and is responsible for keeping them on the sacred land of their birth. I'itoi watches from the summit of Baboquivari Peak as the Tohono O'odham go about their ways.

Water Is the Future

The passage of time brings many changes to both people and the landscape. In portions of the desert, streams once ran year-round with water, which the Tohono O'odham directed into irrigation systems to water their crops. As adjacent cities began to demand more water, deep wells tapped the underground aquifer, gradually lowering the water table to the point where it dried up the rivers and streams and altered the way of life for the Tohono O'odham.

M5 is a beautiful globular star cluster in the summer night sky. It contains more than 100,000 stars and is 30,000 light years from the Earth.

Photo courtesy of Sally and Curt King/Adam Block/NOAO/AURA/NSF

The advance of one culture on the land causes another to recede. In the desert, both groups are eventually dependent on the common element of water. Conserving this precious resource and looking at its wise use should allow both cultures to exist. First, the lesson of balancing our lives with the resources and the environment around us is crucial. The Tohono O'odham people understood the balance of living within the available resources. Perhaps later cultures have not yet learned the necessity of achieving that balance. Beneath your feet lies an enormous underground aquifer that supports life on the surface. Drought cycles have contributed to the depletion of that underground aquifer, resulting in the drilling of deeper and deeper wells. If replenishment of the aquifer fails to occur, cultural changes are inevitable once again.

Be sure to see the work of Tohono O'odham artists, noted for their high quality baskets and pottery, at the trading post just east of the turn to the Kitt Peak Observatory.

Travel Log

- Kitt Peak National Observatory contact information: noao.edu/kpno, 520-318-8726.

- Kitt Peak National Observatory is 56 miles (about 90 minutes) southwest of Tucson on AZ 86. Once you turn south onto AZ 386, it is 12 miles to the summit.

- Kitt Peak is open every day from 9 a.m. to 4 p.m., except Thanksgiving, Christmas, and New Year's days. Three one-hour tours are available each day; call ahead to verify times and to plan your trip (520-318-8726). Admission is free. The special evening programs require advance reservations and special fees apply.

- Be sure to pack a picnic lunch to enjoy the views at the nice picnic area just below the summit. Other things to bring with you include binoculars, hat, sunscreen, camera, and a small flashlight.

8

Meteor Crater

Did you know that each day meteors bombard the Earth? Most of them fall harmlessly into the ocean and many are too small to cause notice. Occasionally, however, a large meteor hits our planet. Arizona is one place where the results of such an impact are perfectly preserved. If you were witness to such an event, it would be an unforgettable moment.

A Visitor from Outer Space

On its fateful course to rendezvous with the planet Earth, a relatively small rock, estimated at half a football field in diameter, silently glides through space. As it encounters the outer layers of Earth's atmosphere, it begins to glow from the heat of resistance. Fiery pieces break off, leaving a trail of fire etched in the sky. The increasing density of the atmosphere begins to slow the speed of the meteor. It is now traveling at a speed that would enable it to travel from the East Coast to the West Coast of the United States in four minutes—exceeding 40,000 miles per hour, 50 times the speed of sound! Estimates place its weight at several hundred thousand tons. For comparison, its estimated width is about the size of the lower parking lot at Meteor Crater's visitor center.

The sonic boom caused by the approaching meteor shatters the silence in the vast desert of the southwest corner of North America. The thundering boom no doubt startles the few animals of this desert landscape.

The violence of the impact is only seconds away. As it slams into the Earth, it throws 300 million tons of rock and dirt into the air. Layers of limestone are instantly pulverized to fine dust. The meteor bores into the Earth, creating a crater 750 feet deep and 4,000 feet wide. The southeast rim of the crater is 150 feet higher than the rest of the rim, suggesting the meteor approached from the northwest. Acting like a giant bulldozer gouging out the Earth, the meteor literally turns the geology of the southeast crater rim upside down, depositing the material from the bottom of the crater along the rim. Within a few minutes, the sound subsides, but the dust lingers for months. The surface of the Earth is left with a massive scar.

All this occurred 50,000 years ago. It would be 40,000 years before humans would begin to explore and populate this region. Today, the crater is about 550 feet deep, having filled in by sediments during the 50,000 years since impact, but the view is still awesome.

Meteor Crater offers the visitor more than you might imagine. For some, it may just be a hole in the ground and is perhaps not worth the admission. Once inside, however, time seems to slip away and your interests grow. A visit can lead to a lifetime of discovery, learning how to read the evidence of these messengers from space, perhaps even joining the search for other craters. It is difficult to visit this place and not direct your gaze into the sky above, wondering if other large, deep-space objects are on an intercept course with our planet. Scientists estimate that meteors the size of the one in Arizona hit the Earth about every 50,000 years. Are we due for another one soon?

Meteor Crater is definitely a place for many discoveries.

Crypto Scene

Understanding the terminology is helpful when discussing these rocky space visitors. Objects traveling through space are *meteoroids*. Once they have entered the Earth's atmosphere, meteoroids become *meteors*. Once they strike the Earth, they become *meteorites*. Their fiery fall to the Earth often cause people to call them "shooting stars."

Comets, on the other hand, travel on predictable elliptical orbits through the solar system. They display a trailing tail of ice and dust particles as they approach the sun, which warms the nucleus of the comet and causes its icy center to evaporate, releasing small dust particles. After passing close to the

An overwhelming sense of quiet surrounds evidence of the tremendous forces released when a meteor slammed into the Earth here.

Hourly guided tours lead visitors along the rim of the crater to Barringer Point. Looking back toward the facilities of the museum provides a human scale to the enormous impact crater.

sun, comets may be flung into deep space beyond the orbit of Pluto. Scientists call the extinct nuclei of comets *asteroids.*

Three types of meteorites exist: the *iron, stony,* and *stony irons.* Iron meteorites survive the entry into Earth's atmosphere the best. Stony and stony irons have a tendency to fragment upon entering the atmosphere. The largest meteorite ever found, the Hoba West Iron, landed in Africa and weighs more than 65 tons. The meteorite that crashed in Arizona was 90 percent iron, with the largest piece remaining weighing 1,406 pounds. The largest iron meteorite discovered in the United States fell in the Willamette Valley of Oregon and weighed more than 15 tons (30,000 pounds).

Would you recognize a piece of a meteorite if you saw it? *Tektites* are by-products from the impact of a meteorite on Earth. These small pieces of fused glass are irregular in shape, sometimes shiny, and usually black, green, or sometimes colorless. Created under tremendous heat and pressure, scientists now believe tektites are the "splash" material from an impact. Moldovite is a green gemstone, found in the former Czechoslovakia, and is a type of tektite.

Research indicates an extremely large meteorite caused the disappearance of the dinosaurs an estimated 65 million years ago. The impact threw so much dust and debris into the atmosphere that it blocked sunlight from reaching the Earth's surface for months or maybe longer, resulting in the loss of 70 percent of the species on Earth, including the plant life and the dinosaurs that depended on them to survive.

Dreams Start Early

Learning about impact craters and meteorites can easily become more than just an interesting hobby. Eugene Shoemaker chased such dreams. He once said, "I had a personal goal that inspired me to begin studying craters on the Earth. I wanted to be the first geologist on the moon." Regrettably, Dr. Shoemaker had a medical condition that precluded him from making his dreamed journey to space. He remained active in training other astronauts for the work of exploring impact craters on the moon, helping them prepare for the exploration of other worlds. Following his death in 1997, as a tribute to his unfailing support of the mission to the moon, Dr. Shoemaker's ashes were placed in a small capsule aboard the Lunar Prospector on its journey to the moon. In this way, he finally realized his dream of reaching the moon, and Dr. Shoemaker will forever be a part of the exploration of space.

While exploring Meteor Crater, it's possible that you'll be following in the footsteps of astronauts. If you visit in the fall, you will observe astronauts training for upcoming missions at Meteor Crater. Astronauts closely study the evidence of impact craters to increase their powers of observation of the surfaces on other worlds great distances from our own. It is crucial to be able to distinguish a volcanic crater from a crater caused by a meteor because it can lead to entirely different interpretations of a planet's history.

Meteor Crater was the first proven impact crater on Earth and has provided tools to help positively confirm other meteorite craters around the Earth and other planets. Fully understanding the shape and patterns of impact craters has helped scientists unlock the secrets of similar formations on the moon and other planets.

Micro Scape

The museum at Meteor Crater is exceptional. Computer-controlled simulations allow visitors to select a type of incoming object—asteroid, comet, or meteor—select the approach speed of the object, and specify the angle of approach. The program runs a simulation and displays what the results might be when the object you selected strikes the earth.

Other exhibits highlight news stories of near misses, when meteorites did crash into the Earth, sometimes causing minor injuries to those unlucky enough to be standing in the wrong place. The museum also includes an excellent film animation of the Arizona meteor, which helps you to understand and appreciate the cataclysmic size of the event and leaves you weighing the consequences of a modern-day event. More than 150 confirmed meteor impact craters have been discovered around the world. Exhibits provide a better appreciation of the global distribution of impact craters and allow an armchair visit to these fascinating sites.

Will another large meteor strike the Earth soon? There is no way to accurately answer that question. However, the Near-Earth Asteroid Tracking (NEAT) program monitors the trajectory of space objects, projecting the potential of them striking the Earth. The Jet Propulsion Laboratory (JPL) and the National Aeronautics Space Administration (NASA) website provide updated information on objects approaching the Earth.

Meteorite Fever

Aside from the obvious crater caused by an impact, we are now accumulating other pieces of evidence to aid in our search and confirmation of meteorite impacts. Because of the tremendous heat and pressures from impacts, scientists reasoned that they should find "shocked rocks" under the

You can drive your own meteor to simulate its impact on Earth. Select the approach speed, angle of impact, and the type of object, and the computer monitor displays the results of such hypothetical collisions.

surface of impact craters. In 1960, Dr. Shoemaker discovered *coesite,* a dense material previously created only in laboratory experiments, in association with meteorite impact craters. Since that initial discovery, another type of extremely dense rock was discovered at Meteor Crater, *stishovite,* almost 70 percent denser than coesite. It takes two million pounds of pressure per square inch to create stishovite. Both of these unusual rock types help us attribute the formation of craters to meteorite impacts.

If you catch the fever for hunting meteorites, here are a few tips to help you on your search: Most meteorites are dark in color due to a fusion crust created on its surface as it passes through the atmosphere. Meteorites may have slight striations on the surface from the effects of the air flowing along its surface. Most are two to three times heavier than rocks of the same size. A magnet will be strongly attracted to a meteorite. Meteorites are generally not rounded and smooth, so look for irregular shapes. Visit a rock shop to see specimens of meteorites so you can develop a mental picture of what they look like.

Thousands of meteors enter Earth's atmosphere every day. Scientists estimate nearly 20,000 tons of rock enter the atmosphere annually, but most of them are too small to survive the fiery descent to the surface. Two-thirds of the Earth's surface is water, so most of the meteorites land harmlessly in the oceans. Nonetheless, prospecting for meteorites is a hobby for many people. The best places to find meteorites are in the desert, with dry lakebeds even a better prospect since few other rocks clutter the field of view. If a meteor fragments upon entry into the atmosphere, the debris forms an elliptical-shaped field, called a "strewn field." Maps of known strewn fields are published and available. Before searching a property, find out who owns it and obtain permission from private landowners to be sure it's OK to search for meteorites.

Tools include a metal detector, shovel, magnet, and small hand lens for examining the surface of potential meteorites. Rare specimens can bring as much as $500 per gram. Owning a piece of rock from another world, however, is the major thrill for people searching the globe for these treasures.

Back in Time Line

Early visitors and scientists to Meteor Crater thought it was a volcanic crater. Others thought it might be a giant blowout in the Earth's surface, caused by escaping gases. They reasoned that if the crater had been caused by a meteorite, where were its remains? Using a magnetic compass, they even walked the interior of the crater, hoping the buried iron would affect the compass needle. The needle did not move, so they concluded that a meteorite did not cause the crater.

In 1902, Daniel Moreau Barringer, a mining engineer and lawyer from Philadelphia, was convinced a meteorite caused the crater. He was also sure that the object survived the crash and the meteorite was still at the bottom of the crater. He and a partner filed a mining claim to recover the iron, anticipating that it would yield a significant return on their investment. After drilling 28 holes in search of the elusive meteorite, they abandoned the effort. Scientists concluded that the meteorite largely disintegrated upon impact. The largest piece ever discovered, the Holsinger Meteorite named in honor of its discoverer, weighed 1,406 pounds and is on display at the Crater Museum. Two other chunks, one weighing 1,050 pounds and another 1,000 pounds, are on display in New York and Chicago.

Although he failed to find the mineral riches he was seeking, Daniel Moreau Barringer managed to convince the world of the scientific value of this spectacular gash in the surface of the Earth. In the scientific community, the crater's official name is the Barringer Crater. The Barringer family continues to manage Meteor Crater today.

Travel Log

- Meteor Crater contact information: meteorcrater.com, 800-289-5898.
- The crater is located 35 miles east of Flagstaff, 5 miles south of I-40 (at exit 233) on an excellent paved road.
- Plan a two- to three-hour visit to Meteor Crater. The film and exhibits are captivating and very informative. Include time for the hour-long walk along the rim and adequate time to sit at the observation points behind the visitor center to contemplate the enormity of the event that created this natural wonder.
- Privately owned, Meteor Crater is a National Natural Landmark and an admission fee applies ($12 for adults, $11 for seniors, $6 for juniors ages 6 to 17). From Memorial Day to Labor Day, Meteor Crater is open 7 a.m. to 7 p.m.; the rest of the year it's open 8 a.m. to 5 p.m. (closed Dec. 25).
- For your rock collection: Look for a tektite or a small piece of a meteorite.

9

Montezuma Castle National Monument

Discovery Zone

Almost like a fortress from a fairy tale, Montezuma Castle silently stands guard over the waters of Beaver Creek. Gone are the voices of the people who lived here and the rhythms of their daily lives and activities. The 20-room pueblo, built over a period of years, features about 2,000 square feet of floor space. If listed in a real estate ad, the only drawback would have been that the front door is 50 feet above the ground! It may only be conjecture, but it would be easy to assume that the prehistoric inhabitants probably experienced a bit of pride in what they built. Montezuma Castle is the best-preserved prehistoric dwelling in the Southwest, with close to 90 percent of the structure consisting of original material.

Montezuma Castle acquired its name from early explorers to the region. Convinced that the 16th-century Aztec king built and inhabited the magnificent cliff dwelling, they applied a name worthy of a king. A quick check of history, however, confirms that the castle existed long before Montezuma was born. Prehistoric Sinagua Indians actually built Montezuma Castle about 900 years ago. In fact, the entire Verde Valley was a population center for the Sinagua. Despite the name given to this band of people (*Sinagua* is Spanish for "without water"), the Verde Valley provided a reliable source of water, which directed the settlement of the Sinagua as well as the Hohokam people before them.

Can you imagine being able to enter the castle today? How do you think its inhabitants managed to climb into their house? The only imaginable method of entering the castle involved the use of rope ladders woven from native plant materials or wooden ladders with the rungs lashed to the upright poles. Narrow ledges, hand and toeholds, and doors allowed access from room to room. Up until 1951, visitors to Montezuma Castle climbed heavy-duty ladders to explore the castle and enjoy the view of the creek below. As foot traffic increased, members of the park staff began to detect damage to the pueblo. As a result, in 1951, park management decided to close the pueblo to the public. Archeologists, who still conduct annual inspections, relate that

Perched 50 feet above the trail, Montezuma Castle is serenely nestled in a limestone alcove.

walking the narrow ledges while trying to both admire the view and watch their step is nerve-racking.

Montezuma Castle was home to an estimated 50 people at a time. If you were able to view the walls on edge, you would notice they are thick at the bottom, tapering toward the top. A waist-high courtyard wall on the uppermost level probably served to protect youngsters from falling over the edge. This outdoor area, sheltered from the intense sunlight and rain, must have been a perfect gathering area, where household chores (such as grinding corn, and weaving mats and sandals) mixed with socializing.

Not far from the Montezuma Castle are the remains of another pueblo, named Castle A by archeologists. The number and diversity of prehistoric dwellings found throughout the Verde Valley point to the likelihood that this region was a significant trade center on a north-south route between the settlements in Mexico and the Hopi Mesas. Many other prehistoric structures are located within a short distance of Montezuma Castle, creating what must have been a bustling community. Nearby irrigation canals, ceremonial mounds, and ball courts all support the conclusion that the prehistoric people who lived in this region were very social and possessed a sophisticated level of architectural skills.

Unlike other prehistoric sites in the Southwest, tree-ring dating of the sycamore trees used as roof timbers provide few specific dates for construction of the castle. The annual growth rings of sycamore trees, which grew in the reliably wet environment of Beaver Creek, were uniform in size, yielding few patterns that matched the beams of other ancient trees used at drier sites. Archeologists resorted to correlating pottery types from Montezuma Castle with pottery types known from dated archeological sites. Their best guess is that the castle saw its major use between A.D. 1150 and A.D. 1350.

Montezuma Castle and the nearby Montezuma Well provide a relaxing break from I-17, serving up an intriguing story, too. Schedule your visit near lunch hour and bring a picnic—the picnic area at Montezuma Well is one of the more inviting ones in the central valley. Lined with old cottonwood trees, the shade and abundant bird activity are a welcome relief on a summer afternoon. The grassy area is a perfect place to toss a Frisbee.

Crypto Scene

Montezuma Well receives less than half the visitation of the castle, yet it has several interesting and curious features to explore. The well is actually a large sinkhole, caused by the collapse of the roof of a cave carved out of the limestone. Wider than the length of a football field, it is 368 feet across and more than 50 feet deep. A free-flowing spring fills the sinkhole with water at a constant 76 degrees and maintains a constant level. Each day one-and-a-half million gallons of water enter the sinkhole—enough to fill 70 average-size swimming pools! The water is not drinkable due to the high level of dissolved minerals, but it is suitable for irrigation purposes.

Understanding the complete story of Montezuma Well is not possible without taking the self-guided trail into the sinkhole to see the *swallet,* a crack in the limestone through which water drains out, and the canal system on the other side. A trail leads to the southwest edge of the sinkhole. At this point, the water disappears through the swallet, travels underground for 150 feet, and emerges outside the sinkhole.

The early Sinagua, and even earlier populations of the Hohokam, took advantage of the emerging water by constructing ditches and canals to move the water to their fields to irrigate their crops—up to a mile from the outlet. During the summer months, this lovely spot is almost a garden, featuring ferns, sycamore trees, and columbines. The mineral-laden water leaves *travertine* deposits, or calcium carbonate, along the walls of the canals, making it appear as if the prehistoric people had deliberately lined the canals.

Wild Things

"Hey, I'll bet the catfish are real whoppers here," visitors say. That would probably be true of these warm waters if not for the high concentration of carbon dioxide at Montezuma Well. The concentration is almost 600 times above normal levels! While not very hospitable to fish, the high concentrations of carbon dioxide provide scientists with a very interesting microenvironment

Montezuma Well invites exploration. Lining the walls of this prehistoric pond are the stone dwellings of the ancient Sinagua, long vanished from the Verde Valley.

to study. Abundant aquatic vegetation, such as algae, feed small shrimp-like amphipods, which in turn become food for leeches. The plant-eating leeches share the well with a few blood-sucking leeches, which probably feed on turtles and muskrats that occupy the water and the edges of the shore. The remarkable aspect of the aquatic environment at Montezuma Well is the gradual evolution each species had to endure to adapt to what might have been a very hostile place to call home.

Back in Time Line

Long before television and even radio, people read adventure tales for excitement. Teenage boys, especially, followed various stories of adventure and exploration in *St. Nicholas* magazine. One issue of the magazine carried a story on Montezuma Well. Writing to increase the suspense of exploration, Charles F. Lummis described Montezuma Well as a "gruesome black lake," adding, "One can wade out a few feet (into the waters of the well) in knee-deep water—if one has the courage in that creepy place—and then, suddenly, as walking from a parapet, step off into the bottomless."

Adding further suspense, Lummis wrote, "I am assured that a sounding line has been sent down three hundred and eighty feet, in a vain attempt to find bottom, and that is easily credible." Of course, the Well is only 50 feet deep, but the hyperbole increased the mystery and certainly the adventure for young readers.

A shady glade offers the heat-weary traveler a brief respite. The picnic area at Montezuma Castle can be a popular spot, especially on weekends.

Water exiting the Montezuma Well travels in prehistoric canals designed to provide vital irrigation to the crops of the Sinagua. Calcium carbonate lines the canal, a travertine deposit built up slowly over time as the water flowed.

Lummis provided very accurate descriptions of the Montezuma Well, too. In painting a word picture of the outlet from the well, he writes, "Here is the outlet of the subterranean stream from the well. From a little hole in the very base of the cliff the glad rivulet rolls out into the light of day, and tumbles heels over head down a little ledge to a pretty pool of the creek. The water of the well is always warmish, and in winter a little cloud of vapor hovers over the outlet."

Perhaps drawing from explorations in other locations, Lummis told young readers of exploring a network of caves by the light of a torch, finding objects from ancient civilizations, and stumbling on steam vents deep inside the complex. Fascinated about the idea of exploring previously unknown destinations, it would be an easy step to imagine yourself as the first explorer to uncover mysteries of scientific value. Lummis succeeded in stirring the imagination about places in the Southwest.

Travel Log

- Montezuma Castle National Monument contact information: nps.gov/moca, 928-567-3322.
- Montezuma Castle National Monument and the Well are about 50 miles south of Flagstaff on I-17; signs mark both exits (exit 289 and exit 293, respectively).
- Bring a picnic lunch for the stop at Montezuma Well (about 11 miles from Montezuma Castle).
- For your rock collection: Look for the Arizona rock argillite, an important prehistoric trade item from a quarry located several miles to the west of Montezuma Castle.

10

Navajo Country

Have you ever visited the Navajo Indian Reservation? Its landscape inspires the romanticism of the West for many Americans; it is a popular destination for Europeans, who commonly visit the region. The landscape is austere and quiet. A sense of tranquility comes over the person standing in its embrace, tracing the large summer clouds across the sky. Many have called it a timeless place. The bottoms of the clouds are pink, reflecting the red rock of the canyons, cliffs, and mesas. To experience its solitude is the initial step toward understanding the soul of the Navajo people, who revere their land and feel deeply connected to it.

When first entering the vast Navajo Indian Reservation, which is larger than the state of West Virginia, few things seem out of the ordinary. You'll see scattered houses with an occasional basketball hoop, a couple of pickup trucks, and a small corral—typical scenes in the Southwest. After a few miles, you may begin to spot a couple of differences. Look more carefully. Do you see any different types of buildings within these isolated ranches? How about the small multisided structure that is on almost every ranch? If your powers of observation are exceptionally keen, you will see another pattern—the doorways to these small, distinctively shaped buildings always face east. This building is the *hogan,* the symbol of the Navajo and central to the Navajo way of life.

The Navajo Indian Reservation covers a good portion of northern Arizona and spills into New Mexico and southern Utah. It is impossible to see it all in a couple of days or even a week. This is especially true if you like to explore and slow down to "Indian time," when intense schedules and rushing around are not as important as living in the present and enjoying the blessings of the beauty surrounding you.

If you are seeking authenticity, consider joining a Navajo family for an evening of storytelling around a campfire and sleeping in a hogan. It will leave a lasting impression. After sunset, silent sentinels of massive buttes and mesas stand distant guard over the flickering light of the fire, and the night sky, undiminished by city lights, almost seems like a blanket of diamonds drawn over your head. Coyotes howl in the distance and the world shrinks to the edge of the light created by the fire. Slowly you can begin to appreciate why the Navajo consider this land their home.

The Hogan

The Navajo word *hooghan* translates to "place home," providing the Navajo with both a sense of place in the universe and a practical home. Usually six- or eight-sided and constructed of mud, logs, stone, and even concrete, depending on the available materials, the construction method itself has remained unchanged since the 1700s. The passage of time has led to some refinements to the hogan, but the basic floor plan remains the same. They are relatively simple to construct, featuring a completely open floor plan. The Navajo were nomadic when they first entered the Southwest; the hogan evolved as they made the transition from a nomadic culture to a more sedentary lifestyle. The Navajo had already made the transition by the time the Spanish entered the territory inhabited by the Navajo in the 1600s, which is why the Spanish named them the "Apache de Navajo" or "Apache of the Cultivated Fields." Although modern houses serve most families today, the traditional hogan is almost universally present for important family events and maintaining a connection with the past.

Tradition dictates the placement of objects—and even the positions people occupy—within the hogan. The door always faces east to receive the first blessings of the new day. The domed roof represents the sky above, the floor represents the earth, and the central fire represents the North Star. To ensure success, healing ceremonies conducted in the hogan require participants to follow a very specific set of rules, especially while chanting or

The sandstone buttes of Monument Valley Navajo Tribal Park have served as the backdrop for many Western movies. Drive the 17-mile scenic loop and see many spectacular formations that can be the backdrop for your own memories.

singing to cure an ailing family member. Traditionally, females sit on the north side of the hogan and the men on the south. The chanter sits on the west side opposite the doorway. Placement of personal possessions within the hogan, including such things as the location of the rug weaver's loom, is also governed by traditions.

The hogan brings back childhood memories of family gatherings, celebrations, sharing meals, and telling stories, and will always remain in the heart of the Navajo people.

"Ya' at' 'eeh"—The Navajo Greeting

Unlike Pueblo cultures like the Hopi, the Navajo live in widely scattered and isolated clusters of houses, often in multigenerational family groups. The Navajo people live independently, within the timeless beauty of the land, moving at a pace of life that reflects the slow changes to the land around them. Some families live without the benefit of electricity and running water. Daily chores include visiting the community wells provided by the tribe for water. In winter, collecting firewood is critical for heating homes and cooking meals. Not many street signs exist on the reservation. A driveway may consist only of a narrow two-track road that leads far from the main paved roads to family homes. The Navajo do not own the property they live on. Instead, they live on "traditional-use" areas, where tribal laws provide them the use of the land. Traditional-use lands belong to the Navajo Tribe; many members of the tribe use much of the reservation's land for traditional purposes such as gathering native plants for ceremonial purposes, collecting different colored sand for sand paintings, or visiting sacred areas. Because of the land-use patterns, it is easy to illegally trespass on traditional-use lands without knowing it. Visitors should stay on established roads or check with tribal offices before venturing into remote areas.

Crypto Scene

A blessing, an experience, and a clean roadside campaign, "Drive in Beauty" signs honor the importance of the land to the Navajo. The dramatic mesas, red buttes, and sheer canyon walls stand out in sharp contrast to the blue sky. The rewards are plenty when the visitor seeks out one of the many destinations on the reservation for a day or two, savoring the experience of anticipating another destination for another day. To rush a visit to the Navajo Country would be to miss the very point of visiting this vast and exceptionally beautiful landscape.

You have so many choices of places and times of year to visit that a little careful planning is essential. Included in the 15 parks within the reservation are national monuments, tribal parks, and several historic sites. If you like one-stop shopping, the sights, sounds, and wonderful Indian food are all featured in one place at the Navajo Tribal Headquarters at Window Rock during the Annual Navajo Nation Fair every September. Billed as the world's largest American Indian fair, with an all-Indian rodeo, mud bog, intertribal powwow, traditional Navajo song and dances, plus the Miss Navajo Nation beauty pageant, the fair captures the fun and spirit of the Navajo. Be sure to sample the blue cornmeal pudding.

Looking for an unusual experience? Take a journey to one or more of the trading posts on the reservation. You're in for an authentic, educational, and rewarding experience. While the historical, cultural, economic, and social focus of the trading post is slowly disappearing—replaced by the mobility of the pickup truck and the lure of shopping in the nearby towns—several posts continue to provide a convenient place for the local Navajo to obtain supplies. Many Navajo continue to establish lines of credit at trading posts by selling rugs, pottery, and jewelry for items they need.

Chapter 5 of this book describes a visit to the Hubbell Trading Post and explains how many Navajo rug patterns are specific to regions of the reservation. Two Grey Hills and Ganado are just two of the rug patterns and trading post names. Post traders often have a hand in helping develop new styles. The trading posts at Lukachukai and Shonto, just two of many that are well-established, include small trading rooms where visitors can find Navajo crafts for sale. The fun is seeking out the locations, visiting with the traders, and watching the activity—not to mention having a drink and a snack. Modern times have influenced the manner in which many Navajo dress on a daily basis, with blue jeans and Western shirts very common. Occasionally, you may see a Navajo woman dressed in the traditional velvet skirt and blouse, wearing her turquoise and silver, coming to trade a rug she has made for items at the trading post. More often, the fancy dress is reserved for the Navajo Nation Fair, special family gatherings, or going to the big city.

The ebb and flow of customers to Shonto Trading Post reflect the rhythms of the Navajo way of life; slowing down to feel them can be a critical part of your experience.

Canyon de Chelly

The beauty of Canyon de Chelly (pronounced d'Shay) lies at the center of the Navajo Nation and in the hearts of the Navajo people. Canyon de Chelly is the Navajo stronghold. The canyon protects Spider Rock, home of Spiderwoman and the creation story. Canyon de Chelly has four distinct seasons, each worthy of a visit. In winter, a light dusting of snow blanketing the quiet canyon, and smoke coming from the occasional hogan, warms the heart. Spring brings forth the blossoms of the peach trees and witnesses the planting of crops. Summer heat, slaked by the gathering thunderstorms and flash floods, slows the pace of life but adds interesting sights, sounds, and smells. Finally, the golden majesty of the cottonwoods in the fall, shimmering in the cooler air, stirs the artist in many people.

Two rim drives provide tantalizing views into the canyons. Looking down to the pastoral farms, groves of trees, small streams, and winding two-track

The 800-foot-tall Spider Rock rises from the floor of Canyon de Chelly. According to the legend of the Navajo, it is home to Spiderwoman, one of the most honored and important deities. She aided the Navajo in destroying the monsters that roamed the land as they traveled from the third world to the fourth world of today.

dirt roads beckon you to the tranquility of a Lilliputian world from your canyon rim perch. It is a safe bet that taking one of the many four-wheel-drive tours of Canyon de Chelly is an experience you will eventually like to repeat. Tours depart regardless of weather. Your adventure may be rather tame—or it might include driving through 12-inch-deep water, carefully avoiding the quicksand found in the canyon bottom. The guide not only points out that 19 vehicles lie completely buried at the mouth of the canyon, but that if you travel into the canyon with your own vehicle (where a guide must accompany you) and become stuck, the towing bill starts at $3,000!

Visitors can hike to a couple of locations in the canyon, but since the canyon is home to several Navajo families, and many archeological sites are found in the canyon, access is restricted and guided tours are the only way many places can be seen. Without a doubt, the assistance of a knowledgeable guide enhances the visit. The only exception to having a permit or tour guide is the trail to White House Ruin. The two-hour round-trip hike descends 500 feet into a canyon and is considered strenuous. Be sure to carry enough water, especially during the summer months.

Up for a Hiking Adventure?

Three prehistoric dwellings are within Navajo National Monument, west of Kayenta on US 160, and north on AZ 564. The prehistoric structures within the park are not from the Navajo culture, but are located within the Navajo Indian Reservation. A highly rewarding but arduous hike is the 8-mile trek to Keet Seel. Discovered in 1895, this Anasazi culture dwelling remains much as it was at the time of discovery, even though abandoned for 700 years. Corn-cobs, broken pottery, sandals, and baskets are scattered about, leaving the impression its inhabitants may have left only months, not centuries, ago.

To enter the dwelling, visitors must climb a wooden ladder. Keet Seel, meaning "broken pottery" in the Navajo language, has 160 rooms. It is the largest cliff dwelling in Arizona. Access is limited to 20 people per day, May through September, and a park ranger must accompany everyone. In fact, the ranger lives near the ancient dwelling around the clock to ensure its protection. Call the Navajo National Monument headquarters for a reservation and to confirm arrangements (928-672-2700). Depending on the time of the year, the hiker fords the same shallow stream many times along the trail to Keet Seel. Your feet will get wet, so wear tennis shoes that will dry or waterproof boots. This hike takes all day and advance planning is critical. Take plenty of water—a gallon per person—and high-energy food. Sun protection and a hat are essential.

A shorter hike to the prehistoric Ledge House, or Betatakin, pueblo is strenuous because the trail descends and ascends 700 feet. Access to Betatakin is granted only with a park ranger and limited to 25 people per day. Carry at least a half gallon of water per person per day. Allow five to six hours for the round-trip. An easier, 1-mile round-trip overlook trail allows for a scenic view of Betatakin from across the canyon.

Understanding the Navajo language, capable of many fine descriptive distinctions, is very difficult. Its unique nature served America during World War II when Navajo soldiers, named the "Code Talkers," conveyed military messages in their native tongue, a code the Japanese were unable to break.

The language serves as the basis for understanding many of their traditions. Navajo customs, ceremonies, the clan system, and even their sense of humor—which is both warm and insightful—remain intricately tied to the language.

Their "First Laugh" rite honors the first time a child laughs aloud. Another fundamental element of the Navajo life is the "Blessingway," a simple yet deeply felt gesture of good hope toward others. The Blessingway ceremony, a rite to ensure good results, is for soldiers going off to war, expectant mothers, and other significant stages in the lives of the Navajo. Performed in the family hogan at least twice a year, the Blessingway reflects how the Navajo teach their children the importance of caring for others.

The Bones of Children

Navajo children learn if they misbehave, Spiderwoman may carry them to the top of Spider Rock, an 800-foot spire in Canyon de Chelly, and devour them. White rock formations at the summit of the spire look like bleached bones and the legend reminds children to listen to their parents. Spiderwoman possessed supernatural powers and assisted the Navajo people in learning how to slay the monsters that inhabited the land as the Navajos emerged into this, the Fourth World. Spiderman, her husband, constructed a loom, upon which Spiderwoman taught the Navajo women to weave their rugs. Spider Rock remains a sacred landmark for the Navajo and visitors can see the formation from the South Rim Drive in Canyon de Chelly National Monument.

The Navajo are a resilient, dynamic, creative, and adaptable people. They migrated south from Canada and were noted warriors. Their language ties them to the Apache Indians, including the Jicarillas, Mescaleros, and White Mountain Apaches. The Navajo show an exceptional ability to grow and learn from others. In meeting the Pueblo people, as they advanced into the Southwest, the Navajo quickly adapted many cultural elements as their own. The clan system evolved from these contacts, as well as the construction of more permanent dwellings and the adaptation of new agricultural techniques. The Navajo adopted sheep from the Spanish, eventually leading to the women weaving spectacular rugs, which have rapidly become collectors' items around the world. The horse, too, came from contact with the Spanish. The art of silversmithing, which evolved from blacksmithing, grew into the famous jewelry of the Navajo men. Their art forms continue to evolve into folk art in which Navajo artists poke a bit of fun at themselves and the modern world that surrounds them. For example, art may depict traditionally dressed Navajos riding motorcycles and airplanes, or the modern world reflected in the lenses of sunglasses as the Navajo absorb the world.

While the Navajo have moved steadily into the modern world, many things have not changed. Those critical pieces of their culture left unchanged have provided the Navajo with a strong self-image and inner strength that keeps them unique. Exploring their reservation and understanding their cultural inheritance and traits are what makes this adventure truly awesome.

Travel Log

- Navajo Country contact information: navajo.org, navajonation-fair.com.

- The Navajo Reservation occupies almost the entire northwest corner of Arizona, plus eastern New Mexico and southern Utah. Depending on your destination in the reservation, it is best to consult a map when planning a trip. One key road is US 191, 49 miles east of Holbrook, at exit 333, which places the visitor in the heart of the western portion of the reservation.

- Obtain a copy of the Indian Country map at Arizona convenience stores, book stores, or AAA to explore trading post locations.

- Obtain hiking permits for backcountry trips from the Navajo Parks and Recreation Department in Window Rock, Arizona (928-871-6647).

- Stay overnight in an authentic hogan, located in Monument Valley at the foot of Black Mesa. For information about hogans, make local inquiries.

- Watch the clock, especially in summer, since the Navajo Reservation observes Daylight Savings Time.

- A few cultural notes: As with the Hopi people, ask before taking pictures of the Navajo; often, a fee is expected. Raised to be very polite, the Navajo avoid eye contact, which they consider impolite. Other cultural traits, ingrained since childhood, include a certain reserve when talking with strangers. These customs are not a sign of disinterest or disrespect.

Visitors return from viewing Antelope House pueblo, a prehistoric dwelling of the Anasazi people. The Anasazi left their canyon homes about 700 years ago and the Navajo entered the Canyon de Chelly area about 300 years ago.

11 Petrified Forest National Park

Discovery Zone

Hiking in Petrified Forest may be a different experience than suggested by its name. Some visitors to Petrified Forest arrive at the park with the idea that they will be walking within the standing but fossilized remains of an ancient woodland—a stone forest. However, visitors quickly discover that identifying a standing tree, petrified or living, is a challenge in the almost lunar landscape of the park. A real sense of discovery occurs when their walk quickly reveals a landscape littered with the fallen giants of a 225-million-year-old Triassic period forest.

This park protects the largest concentration of petrified wood known in the world. In this outdoor laboratory, trails wind amongst the scattered remains of ghosts from another time. What did this ancient forest look like? How did such large trees grow in such a stark landscape? Did this area look dramatically different than it does now? The clues to answering these questions surround you, but caution is advised, because the answer to one question might lead to several more. Step into the mystery of Petrified Forest National Park and get into the Triassic spirit. Imagination is part of the fun and the key to unlocking the landscape of Petrified Forest National Park.

A Walk in the Stone Forest

A young visitor, walking among the colorful fallen logs on a self-guided trail in the park, calls back to her parents, "Hey, look at me, I'm hiking in the forest!" Her imagination has indeed transported her back in time to the once tropical world in which these huge—and now petrified— tree trunks once reached for the sky. Most of the logs you will see are the remains of cone-bearing coniferous trees, usually evergreens. They reached diameters of up to 10 feet at the base and grew up to 200 feet tall. You may discover the rare base of a tree protruding from the ground, which suggests that the slow process of turning to stone occurred just where the tree stood. More often, the trees were tossed and rolled in flooded streambeds, leaving them randomly scattered about. The final resting place of the logs may help you to imagine the ancient forest and the landscape. As you will learn, the journey from a living monarch of the forest to a stone artifact from an ancient past has as much to do with luck as it does history.

Scattered over the landscape, fallen trees are now part of a stone forest. Explore the Giant Logs Trail at the south end of Petrified Forest National Park.

Paleo Scene

The landscape of Petrified Forest National Park you see today bears little resemblance to the prehistoric scene of 225 million years ago, known as the Late Triassic period. Can you guess why this area looked so different long, long ago? Would you think it possible that where you are standing today was once at the equator? How could that be?

North America was once part of a supercontinent named *Pangaea* (Greek for "all lands"). This super continent started to break apart about 200 million years ago. The resulting smaller continents "float" as plates on a layer of molten rock called the mantle. The plates drift in different directions. They move at extremely slow rates, sometimes only 1 to 2 inches per year, occasionally colliding with one another. This movement continues even today. One such collision zone occurs in California as the Pacific Plate rubs against the North American Plate, resulting in earthquakes. Sometimes one plate overrides the adjacent plate, forcing up mountain ranges along the zone of collision. All of the continents ride these giant plates, which cover the Earth like the cracked shell of a hard-boiled egg. The geologic term *plate tectonics* explains the movement of these plates and scientific measurements track their progress over the globe.

The plate that carries North America—and the area destined to become Petrified Forest National Park—began to drift gradually north from the equatorial latitudes. Because of its once southerly location, the area had a warmer and moisture-rich equatorial climate, creating a lush tropical forest environment. Scientists estimate that this part of North America, which eventually became Arizona, was east of present-day Panama, somewhere between Africa and South America. You might say that Arizona has come a long way!

Standing at the Equator

Imagine yourself standing in that primeval forest, surrounded by 200-foot-tall trees in warm moist air with hardly a breeze stirring. Even the smaller plants would be strange to you. Some ferns and a few other plants might remind you of your 21st-century world, but for the most part you are in a very different world. Dinosaurs were just beginning their developmental journey to eventually reach a point of dominance in the prehistoric world. Insects were abundant, but no mammals roamed the land and no birds filled the skies. Geologists and paleontologists suggest the region was a low-lying, stream-braided, relatively flat floodplain—generally, the impression was of a swampy environment.

As you stand on the trail at Crystal Forest, with numerous large petrified trees lying all around, can you imagine this ancient land? It is remarkable that these forest giants survived to see, once again, the sunlight of a world 225 million years older. Their journey into your world has been a long one, filled with many obstacles and overwhelming odds. As you explore the park, be sure to give fossils the respect they deserve for having survived a long odyssey, both in time and distance.

Yet, their journey is not over yet. While fossils may not appear fragile, the forces of wind, rain, and sunlight continue to threaten their existence. Each passing year takes its toll on these exposed time travelers. Humans also endanger these gifts from the past. Hundreds of pounds of fossils disappear from the park each year, taken by visitors who think they must have a piece of time. At the current rate of theft, visitors in the not-too-distant future may not be able to see any petrified wood at all in the park. It is critically important that you leave everything here as you found it, so that others can enjoy it, too. Theft of petrified wood from the park is one of the biggest challenges the park faces today, so please do your part to keep this ancient forest in place as a window into the past.

The Dawn of Dinosaurs

During the Triassic period of the Mesozoic era, the ancient forests of Petrified Forest flourished. Overall, the Mesozoic era was the Age of Reptiles. It lasted from 200,000 million years ago until about 70,000 million years ago. While the Triassic period did witness the early development of the dinosaur, for the most part dinosaurs were still in the future as the forest matured. The Triassic period experienced a great deal of climatic change, so numerous

The almost barren landscape of the Painted Desert, located north of I-40, changes colors with the different angles of sunlight. Early morning and late afternoon are the best times to view and photograph this portion of the park.

photo courtesy of PFMA and National Park Service

species evolved quickly and then disappeared—almost as quickly. The Jurassic period and later the Cretaceous period followed the Triassic period.

Fossil remains of prehistoric reptiles are not in great abundance at Petrified Forest National Park. The crocodile-like *Rutiodon* is one exception. This fierce predator moved on land as well as in the water, snapping up fish and anything else it might capture in its long, narrow snout. Protected by bony plates on the body and along its tail, the Rutiodon could remain submerged for long periods because its nostrils were on top of its head, almost like a snorkel. The only evidence of its presence would have been its two eyes and the nostrils above the water. As the prehistoric environment changed, the Rutiodon, with its ability to live on dry land and in the water, was one of the more successful species in the Late Triassic period because it could adapt to the changing environment.

One impressive and relatively large plant-eating animal was the *Placerias,* which was about the size of a medium-size hippopotamus. Based on the size of its bones, scientists estimate it probably weighed about 2,000 pounds. Large numbers of fossil remains found in quarries within Petrified Forest National Park suggest to scientists that the Placerias probably traveled in herds while roaming the landscape. Their tusks, found on a number of skulls, helped to turn up the soil in efforts to find plant roots and tubers to eat. Or, perhaps the horns came in handy in combat with other Placerias. Visitors can meet a replica of the Placerias face to face in the Rainbow Forest Museum, at the southern entrance to the park.

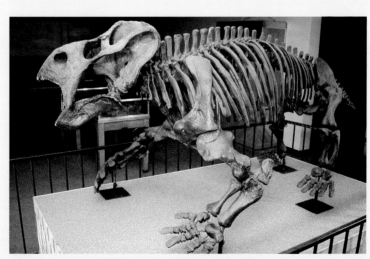

The plant-eating Placerias roamed the earth about 225 million years ago. This lifesize replica can be seen at the Rainbow Forest Museum.
photo courtesy of PFMA and National Park Service

Crypto Scene

Chances of a plant or animal becoming part of the fossil record are remote. The conditions for the fossilization process must be just right—and after that, the fossil must be discovered by a paleontologist to make it into our world. The discovery of a fossil is an exciting moment because scientists understand the extraordinary odds in making a successful journey through the time tunnel from past to present.

Several different types of fossils exist. Small plant or animal parts, flattened by the weight of the mud or other fine-grained sediments, create "compression fossils." Gradually accumulating sediments entomb the plants or animals. Deposited in layers, sediments frequently split along the same layer, revealing the minute details of early plant seeds, leaves, stems, and even tiny pollen grains. Compression fossils have revealed fine details, such as prehistoric feathers and fish scales. Fossil impressions look like they are painted on the surface of the rock. The thin black film is carbon, one of the building blocks of plant and animal tissue. Perhaps not as dramatic as articulated dinosaur bones, compression fossils yield a wealth of critical information about the prehistoric environment.

Once scientists identify plant remains through fossils, the prehistoric environmental conditions come into focus. The "paleo" scene gradually emerges into our view. Several varieties of ferns occur among the more than 200 species of fossil plants identified through compression fossils. The delicate details found in compression fossils show small spines on stems and hair on the surface of leaves, enabling scientists to catalog the variety of plant species. Insects, including beetles and the ancestor of the modern cockroach, also find their way into the present as compression fossils. In addition to compression fossils, scientists study "trace fossils," which are not the fossilized remains of a plant or animal itself but simply a sign of its existence. Prehistoric footprints, insect borings, and trackways are types of trace fossils that are found throughout the world.

Forest to Fossil

The process of a living organism gradually turning into stone must occur under ideal conditions. The type of fossil most visitors are familiar with is the petrified fossil. Starting the process as a large tree trunk or the skeleton of a prehistoric animal, the first step is for the plant or animal to come to an undisturbed resting place, because fossil formation is a slow process. Second, quick burial in sand or mud is essential in order to eliminate oxygen. Water is important for fossil formation, because the silica and other minerals dissolved in water gradually replace all the organic matter in the plant and animal. Typically, little internal detail of the living organism is preserved because minerals have replaced all the organic matter. Fossilization in this manner is the most common. As you might guess, fossilized plants and animals are several times heavier than the original plant or animal. Having turned to stone, the "trees" are very heavy, weighing 170 pounds per cubic foot.

Permineralization is another type of petrification. This process preserves much more detail because the individual cells and spaces between cells fill with minerals, resulting in microscopic detail of plant and animal remains. The tan and brown petrified logs, which look very much like modern wood logs, are permineralized logs.

Why are there so many different colors in petrified wood? The type and quantity of the replacing minerals dictate the colors found in fossils. Silica, commonly found in sand, is very abundant in the Chinle Formation in Petrified Forest National Park and yields most of the park's petrified wood. Silica is white and reveals itself as quartz. (The Chinle Formation is one of the most conspicuous geologic formations in the park. Its colorful bands of rocks preserve most of the trees of the petrified forests and also forms much of the Painted Desert in the northern portions of the park.)

Look closely at the cavities within the petrified wood. Quartz, the most abundant mineral, is usually clear. Add a little manganese dioxide, leaching out from volcanic rock, however, and quartz with purple and blue colors results. *Hematite,* or oxidized iron, creates the red and pink hues. Green, on the other hand, is another from of iron, which forms in the absence of oxygen. This type of iron is common in meteorites. Pyrite, sometimes called "fool's gold," creates a black color when exposed to organic carbon in plant and animal tissue. Yellow, brown, and orange colorations result from a hydrated iron oxide called *goethite.* Petrified wood reflects all the colors of the rainbow and close examination with a hand lens will further reveal the delicate nature of this spectacle.

Why are no branches, bark, or twigs attached to the logs? Research indicates that most of the logs that eventually turned to stone must have tumbled and rolled repeatedly in flash floods, removing everything from the tree's surface. Close examination of the trunks reveals the knots where branches attached to the trunks. Less frequently, you may find the stumps of large trees, almost as if a lumberjack had cut them. Can you solve the mystery of why, in some cases, the logs have broken into such uniform lengths?

Micro Scape

There are many ways to enjoy the beauty of Petrified Forest National Park. If you can visit early in the morning or late in the afternoon, the colors of the distant buttes enhanced by the low angle of light, and the shadows cast by these same buttes across this stark landscape, enrich the splendor of the desert landscape. In winter, a light dusting of snow provides a wonderful contrast with the banded and pastel layers of distant formations. Thunderstorms in mid to late summer produce towering cumulus cloud formations, casting long shadows over far-off buttes and plateaus, adding the thrill of a summer downpour. When visiting the park during any weather extremes, take the necessary

The close collaboration of artist and scientist yields the best estimation of what the landscape of the region looked like 225 million years ago. The region that became Petrified Forest was much closer to the equator then and the higher temperatures and humidity fostered a dramatically different environment.

Illustration by Mary Parrish (technical direction by Dr. Sydney Ash), courtesy of PFMA and NPS

Contrast the artist's impression of the ancient landscape above to what you see today. As you explore the park, try to imagine how different the world of over 200 million years ago must have been.

Prehistoric people used blocks of petrified wood in the construction of their pueblo, probably unaware of the origin of the colorful stones. Agate House is located at the end of a short trail at the southern end of the park. Its builders not only used the beautiful stone in its construction but also selected a site with a view.

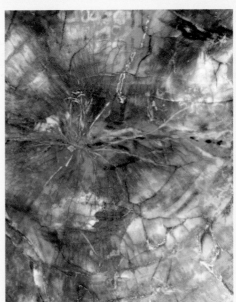

A rainbow in stone, this polished cross-section of a petrified tree reveals the lacy patterns and exquisite colors found in the preserved trees. Although lacking the fine detail seen in the permineralization process, this replacement type of petrification is almost like impressionistic art.

photo courtesy of PFMA and National Park Service

Colorful petrified wood is found in the many-hued layers of the Chinle Formation in Petrified Forest National Park.

photo courtesy of PFMA and National Park Service

precautions from the hazards of flash floods, lightning, and extreme temper-atures. Seeing the park on the edges of day and night, calm and storm, winter and summer, serves to create vivid memories.

Slightly more than half of Petrified Forest National Park's 93,500 acres is federally designated wilderness. In fact, it was the first designated wilderness in a national park area. Keeping the imprint of human activity to an abso-lute minimum is the key ingredient to preserving the quality of these areas.

For an introduction to these undisturbed areas, take a hike to Onyx Bridge. The petrified log bridge spans a side canyon from Lithodendron Wash. If place names cause you to dream of new discoveries, explore Angel's Garden. Or, detour to ancient petroglyphs, a short distance up another wash. Be prepared for wilderness ventures, no matter what the season. Obtain a free permit from the National Park Service before entering the designated wilderness and review the special regulations prior to entry. Permits must be obtained at least one hour before the park closes and are issued at the Rainbow Forest Museum, Painted Desert Inn Museum, and the Painted Desert Visitor Center. If you want to add to the adventure, plan to include an overnight camping trip, an experience you will not soon forget. Leaving civilization behind, if even for 24 hours, can revitalize the soul.

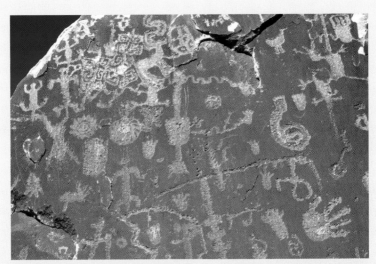

Are these symbols prehistoric doodling, art, clan symbols, or just a form of early written communication? Archeologists are not certain what these petroglyphs are trying to tell us. Do you have any ideas? Photo courtesy of PFMA and National Park Service

Back in Time Line

As with much of the Southwest, evidence of prehistoric people abounds in Petrified Forest National Park. Whether the early dwellers of the Southwest ever recognized the fossil evidence all around them, we will never know. Yet, they incorporated petrified wood in the construction of their dwellings as seen at Agate House in the southern portion of the park. Other prehistoric dwellings dot the landscape, along with petroglyph sites, stone artifacts, and pottery.

The patterns of habitation here reflect those of the region. Several cultures flourished as the weather patterns allowed. The Mogollon and the Anasazi, collectively known as the ancestral Puebloans, were the principal prehistoric people who lived in the area, but each retreated or disappeared 600 years ago, a change generally thought to be linked to drought conditions.

Roughing It, Deluxe

Seeing the prehistoric dwellings and the petroglyph sites adds a human dimension and scale to a visit to the park. The park also preserves reminders of more modern people who ventured into and explored this colorful world. What was it like exploring Petrified Forest National Park in the 1920s, 1930s, and 1940s? The automobile was not yet common, and the hardships to reach this isolated destination discouraged many while attracting some. To travel to the region, tourists took a train into nearby Winslow and then boarded large touring cars to see the sights.

The Painted Desert Inn, which started out as The Stone Tree House, offered visitors lunch and a cool drink while they admired the colorful changing landscape of the Painted Desert. The dwelling gradually evolved over the next several years, as travel in private cars increased along US 66. Lodging was now available, along with more elaborate meals. Take a moment or two to linger on the patio of the Painted Desert Inn, especially late in the afternoon, and imagine not being compelled to rush to another destination before nightfall. Look back to the days when the Painted Desert Inn might have been your luxurious accommodations for the night. As the shadows deepen across the multihued hills with the approach of sunset, you may catch a glimpse of a full moon rising, and as the dusk settles into darkness, the coyotes begin to howl. In the 1940s, this was roughing it, deluxe. The Painted Desert Inn, on the north side of I-40 not far from park headquarters, is undergoing restoration, enabling visitors to appreciate the architectural details and the refinements of another era.

Travel Log

- Petrified Forest National Park contact information: nps.gov/pefo, 928-524-6228.

- Petrified Forest National Park is 26 miles east of Holbrook on I-40, at exit 311. Or, take US 180 southeast from Holbrook for 19 miles to the south entrance of the park.

- Bring a hand lens to see the structural detail of petrified wood.

- Binoculars are essential for looking at far-off details of the vastness of the landscape.

- A quick study of the Indian Country map offers many alluring side trip destinations, often on unimproved roads.

- Make local inquiries about road conditions and be sure to include sufficient water and snacks in case a sudden summer thunderstorm closes the roads.

- For your rock collection: Petrified wood is the official state fossil; you can buy a piece from one of the many rock shops you see on your way to the park.

12 Pima Air & Space Museum

Discovery Zone

Few things reflect the indomitable spirit of human endeavors as well as flight. Even standing motionless on the ground, airplanes stir our imagination. The world celebrated the first century of flight in 2003. Since the first daring leap into the air in 1903, on the windswept dunes of Kitty Hawk, North Carolina, we have witnessed an evolution of a tremendous diversity of aircraft. Although not everyone can be a pilot, just about all of us feel the thrill of walking around airplanes. The Pima Air & Space Museum boasts more than 250 of the most important aircraft in history, but it really does not end there.

Aircraft "are artifacts of our culture in much the same way that clay pots and arrowheads are artifacts of ancient cultures," says James Stemm, curator at the Pima Air & Space Museum. "Each aircraft in our collection tells us a lot about technology of flight at the time it was designed."

The Boeing B-52A on display is the very same aircraft that carried the X-15 rocket plane to the edges of space. Many astronauts, including Neil Armstrong, the first astronaut to walk on the moon, flew the X-15. Because

This B-52A carried the X-15 rocket plane under its right wing to 45,000 feet above the Earth. Then the X-15 was released and eventually reached an altitude of 217,000 feet.

the X-15 burned fuel at such a high rate, the B-52A carried it beneath its wing to 45,000 feet before releasing it to accelerate to six times the speed of sound. The flights tested both the aircraft and the pilot for the challenges of the manned space flight ahead. The B-52A aircraft was but a platform for humans to reach the stars, enabling us to test the boundaries of new technology and build our knowledge. A scale model of the X-15 is in the Space Exploratorium building.

A special story is associated with almost every aircraft on display at the museum. The oldest aircraft in the collection is the Fleet Model 2 biplane, built in 1929. The latest is the SR-71 Blackbird. Be prepared to spend a little time with these old friends and marvel at the advances in design and engineering.

Crypto Scene

"Space Station, this is mission control. Over."
"Mission Control, this is the space station. Over."
"We have a message for the Life Support Team. Over."
"We are ready to receive. Over."

How would you like to train for a space shuttle mission? The dialogue you just read between the Mission Control Center and crew aboard a simulated space shuttle is real. It is part of a carefully crafted mission script for youngsters simulating one of several different space missions.

The Pima Air & Space Museum supports one of 46 Challenger Learning Centers across the nation. It offers an assortment of special programs designed for school groups, including Voyage to Mars, Return to the Moon, and Rendezvous with a Comet. The simulators have computer-equipped Mission Control and Space Station areas. "Aboard" the mission, there are eight workstations that crews must learn and staff for their mission. These stations include Life Support, Medical, Data, Navigation, Probe, Isolation, and Communication. The networks of Challenger Centers serve as a living memorial to the crew of the 51 L Challenger Space Shuttle.

The Challenger Center of the Southwest has mini-missions, lasting 90 minutes, for ages eight and up, plus Inter-Generational Space Day Camps, in which any adult-child combination can register as a team and prepare to fly a mission.

The Rendezvous with a Comet simulation presents mission crews with a little extra excitement: " . . . their goal is to successfully plot a course to rendezvous with a comet and to launch a probe to collect scientific data on the object. What may seem like a routine exploration is sprinkled with lots of surprises and emergencies, giving students first-hand insight into teamwork and problem solving." A trained specialist with the Challenger Center guides the mission, constantly monitoring the crew's performance and keeping the crew on task.

President John F. Kennedy liked the DC-6 aircraft because it was capable of landing and taking off on shorter runways than the Boeing 707 presidential aircraft. The plane went on to serve three presidents. Visitors can tour the inside of this aircraft, which includes the custom armchair used by JFK.

Tucson is very fortunate to host one of the Challenger Learning Centers and the programs are very popular. Drop in to see if you would like to make a simulated trip into outer space—it could be really cool!

Micro Scape

Aircraft restoration is an interesting profession. At the Pima Air & Space Museum, restoration work stops short of bringing the airplanes to operational condition. Museum managers decided that it might be too risky to fly these irreplaceable airplanes and the cost associated with making them airworthy is very high. Instead, they spend available funds on protecting and preserving a larger number of aircraft for the future rather than restoring them to operational condition. For the cost of one full restoration to flight-worthy condition, the museum can preserve several airplanes.

Volunteers not only help museum guests get the most out of their visits, they are critical to helping rebuild airplanes for display. Some of the planes arrive in the back of dump trucks and flatbed trailers. Most people's initial reaction is that the trucks are loaded with nothing but scrap metal or junk. Nevertheless, to the eyes of a trained aircraft restoration specialist, the piles of junk you and I might see are the raw materials of a historic artifact of our aviation history—and part of a dream of bringing the planes back to their former glory.

A few aircraft do arrive at the Pima Air & Space Museum in better condition than a pile of scrap metal. Take a moment to visit the Executive Aircraft display to climb aboard the forerunner to Air Force One, the Presidential airplane. A guided tour of the airplane used by Presidents Dwight D. Eisenhower, John F. Kennedy, and Lyndon B. Johnson is available daily. Parked next to it is the Lockheed Constellation, or Connie. The one on display, the oldest one in existence, served as the workhorse of early commercial aviation in the 1940s and 1950s. Its distinctive three-tail arrangement made the Connie easily recognizable around the world.

Back in Time Line

With more than 250 historically significant aircraft on display, it is a challenge to pick out a favorite. Three aircraft stand out more than the others do—the first because of its contribution to a nation at war and the other two because of their unusual shapes.

The Flying Fortress

Within the 390th Bomb Group Memorial Museum building stands a magnificent old war bird, the B-17G Super Fortress Bomber from World War II. There were 12,731 B-17s built and they provided the airpower that helped the United States win the Second World War.

No other aircraft faced such tremendous punishment in bombing raids over Germany as the B-17. Often returning to base with three of its four engines not working, large pieces of its tail section missing, or unable to lower its landing gear, the plane brought its crew back safely, defying all odds. Many others were not as fortunate. Enemy aircraft or antiaircraft fire from the ground below shot off entire wings or riddled them with so many bullet holes they could no longer fly. At the beginning of the war, these bombers and their crews faced German fighter planes alone, because our Air Force did not have fighter aircraft with sufficient fuel range to escort the bombers all the way to Germany and back from bases in England. Nearly half of all the B-17 bombers flying missions over Germany were shot down. In one raid alone, 120 aircraft were lost, each with a 10-man crew.

Completely restored and protected by the crew members who flew her, the B-17 in the 390th Bomb Group hangar is one of the few aircraft at the Pima Air & Space Museum that is airworthy. However, with so few of these remarkable aircraft remaining, it is unlikely she will ever feel the wind beneath her wings again. The love the crew members have for this airplane is readily apparent. Like looking after an old friend, they stand vigil to protect her as she did them. It is hard to explain why so much metal, rubber, wire, and glass brings out these emotions, but it is easy to believe that, had any of us made the same harrowing journeys as these men did, our respect for the airplane would be the same as theirs.

Climb the ladder to view the entire interior length of the lovingly restored Flying Fortress, I'll Be Around. *Bomb bay doors are open for inspection, too.*

The B-17G, equipped with twelve 50-caliber machine guns, was dubbed the Flying Fortress by a newspaper reporter. Despite its heavy armament, the bombers usually flew in very tight box formations, giving themselves added protection from enemy fighters. Although the B-17G is not large by today's standards, it was a fierce fighting machine in its day. It had a maximum speed of 300 miles per hour at 30,000 feet elevation. The nine- to 10-man crews had to use oxygen masks for altitudes above 10,000 feet and electrically heated suits to protect themselves against the cold temperatures, which might reach 50 degrees below zero at extreme altitudes.

The plane was remarkably stable to fly, but the controls often had to have 100 pounds of pressure applied for turns and banking. Because of this, the B-17 was a young pilot's airplane. Carefully examine the belly gun turret. This gun position was one of the most dangerous in the aircraft. The gunner was essentially outside the aircraft, exposed to enemy fire, and the turret ball had to be in exact position for the gunner to exit through a small hatch at the top. Often, enemy fire damaged the rotating mechanism, preventing the turret from rotating to the exit position. The gunner had to wait until the airplane returned to base to get out of the turret.

The Sled

Maybe because of its thin and flat look, the SR-71 earned the nickname The Sled. On the other hand, perhaps its pilots felt as if they were riding a rocket sled. Either way, the SR-71 is poetry in motion. The more common name

Known as The Sled, the SR-71 Blackbird is one of the sleekest aircraft ever produced. Aside from the recently retired Concorde, it is the only aircraft that can sustain supersonic speeds for five to eight hours.

for the world's fastest spy plane is the Blackbird. Its distinctive silhouette, exceptional speed, and early stealth technology still attract people today, even though it was first flown in the early 1960s. The Blackbird still holds the world's speed record for an operational military aircraft at more than 2,100 miles per hour. In 1990, it flew from Los Angeles, California, to Washington, D.C., in 1 hour, 4 minutes, and 19.89 seconds. It still holds all the world's records for the highest flying and fastest assembly-line produced aircraft ever made. Produced in limited numbers, the only plane that is faster is the X-15 rocket plane.

With innovative technology—including a titanium metal skin to withstand temperatures of 400 degrees plus tires filled with nitrogen and made with powered aluminum embedded in the rubber to endure the hot temperatures of high-speed landings—the SR-71 Blackbird still sets the standard for high performance.

Pilots of the SR-71 wore space suits identical to those of space shuttle astronauts, since this aircraft operated at the edges of space, above 80,000 feet. To prepare the pilots for the long missions and high altitudes, they ate a special, high-protein, low-residue diet. Once suited up, pilots breathed pure oxygen to drive nitrogen out of the bloodstream to avoid the "bends" when descending from high altitudes.

The SR-71 was a very sophisticated aircraft to fly. After starting the engines, the pilot moved the aircraft to the end of the runway to commence the preflight checklist. It took the two-man crew about 25 minutes to complete the checklist. The SR-71 usually takes off with a light fuel load to reach altitude quickly. Once there, the pilot's first obligation is to meet the KC-135Q air tanker for its first in-flight refuel. Topped off with fuel, the SR-71 can fly

Despite its unusual balloon-shaped fuse-lage, the Super Guppy was relatively easy to fly, according to pilots. Of five built, only one Super Guppy remains on duty, serving NASA.

about an hour at its cruising speed of Mach 3.2 before it needs another refuel. Described as a flying gas tank, since most of the space in the fuselage is dedicated to six large fuel tanks, the SR-71 gulps fuel, one of the reasons it was retired early.

Flying at three times the speed of sound creates unusual problems. One specific challenge is dealing with the heat of the aircraft as it collides with air molecules. The inside of the canopy reaches temperatures in excess of 200 degrees. The nose of the SR-71 can reach 800 degrees and the average temperature over the entire aircraft is more than 450 degrees, the same temperature you heat the oven to for baking a pie! On more than one occasion, the plane was still so hot that it set off the automatic fire suppression system in the plane's hangar!

Super Guppy

Finally, check out the distinctively shaped airplane called the Super Guppy. You certainly will not miss seeing this oversize airplane—it almost looks as if it couldn't possibly fly. The Guppy hauled components of the Saturn V rocket engine to Florida and even carried the Hubbell Telescope to Florida to be loaded on the Space Shuttle for launch into orbit. The Super Guppy (SG) is a specialty aircraft, designed to carry 20 tons of cargo at 300 miles per hour. Modified to a diameter of 25 feet and a length of 94 feet, the first Guppy started life as a C-97 J Stratocruiser, or Boeing 377. One limitation of the modified Stratocruiser was that its cargo floor width was only a little less than 9 feet, which presented a problem for flying wide cargo. Despite its ungainly size and shape, pilots say the plane handles very well. The only SG ever built stands here today.

The SG was so useful that a second generation of Guppies was built from scratch. Designated the Super Guppy Turbine (SGT), the plane grew to 111 feet in length and the cargo floor increased to 13 feet. The planes were able to carry an additional 14,000 pounds of cargo—a total of 54,500 pounds, or more than 27 tons! The new turbine engines gave the SGT greater lift, cruising speed, and altitude capabilities. One SGT remains in the service of the National Aeronautics and Space Administration (NASA).

Travel Log

- Pima Air & Space Museum contact information: pimaair.org, 520-574-0462.
- Pima Air & Space Museum is located at 6000 East Valencia Road, Tucson, just east of I-10, at exit 267.
- The Pima Air & Space Museum is open seven days a week, 9 a.m. to 5 p.m., year-round, closing only for Thanksgiving Day, Dec. 25, and a training day in September.
- The Challenger Learning Center of the Southwest offers a wide variety of programs. Contact them directly at 520-574-0462 for specifics on potential school program missions, one of the "flights" available to the public, or the special adult-child programs.

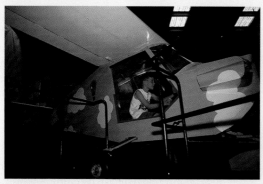

This kid-sized replica of a small private plane is part of the museum in Hangar 1, which also provides an overview of the history of flight and an excellent bookstore dedicated to flying and historical aircraft.

Visitors can view the flight controls of the Presidential Aircraft, a military version of the DC-6. The white handles control the four engines, one set for the pilot and another set for the co-pilot.

13

Queen Mine, Bisbee

Are you ready for a journey into the earth? The town of Bisbee, working with the owners of the Queen Mine, set the stage for underground exploration and adventure into a once-active copper mine. Retired miners lead groups down the main shaft, using an electric locomotive to pull passenger cars into the mine while sharing tales along the way about the years they spent toiling beneath the surface of the earth. Visitors will learn how dynamite charges were set to loosen just the right amount of rock, and see the methods used for shoring up and pulling ore from the mine with square sets and stoping.

The miners are very safety conscious and provide an excellent overview of the evolution of mining techniques and how safer mining techniques developed over the years. It was a hazardous business—for the workers on the day shift, working underground, days and weeks would go by without ever seeing sunlight. In 1885, miners earned $3.50 per day, which might go up or down, depending on the price of copper. Chasing the rich copper veins, life was an endless cycle of drilling, blasting, loading oar cars, and hauling rock to the surface. Despite the many hardships and backbreaking work, many miners continue to speak fondly about their work underground, enjoying the opportunity to share the experiences with people. Bring a light jacket as temperatures in the mine are around 47 degrees.

Dressing for the Part

No adventure or exploration is complete without the right wardrobe. A bright yellow rain slicker, hard hat, and a battery-powered lamp outfit you for the next hour or so. The original changing shed is now the museum, ticket office, and central wardrobe . . . almost like being on a Hollywood movie set.

Once suited up, everyone climbs aboard cars pulled by the Trolley Motor, the same one used to pull ore cars in and out of the mine. The journey will take you about 1,500 feet into the mine on the narrow rails. The tour guide goes over the safety rules before beginning the journey into the mine. Then, with the ring of a bell, the guide announces to all passengers that they are about to get underway.

In the early days, mining did not have the many conveniences developed in later years. Underground fires, caving ground, dim candlelight, and accidental dynamite explosions were just a few of the daily hazards facing early miners. When candlelights were the principle source of light in mining, the flickering flame also tipped off the miners to the presence of carbon dioxide or "black damp." When the candles started to flicker, miners usually vacated the mine immediately to avoid exposure to the deadly gas.

Copper ore from the Queen Mine had a yield of about 23 percent, considered very rich. In the early days, mules carried the copper ore out of the mine. The ore cars, which weighed 1,000 pounds empty, weighed about 2,500 pounds fully loaded. Assigned to specific levels, mules frequently stayed in the mines for long periods. The mules even had underground barns in one of the side shafts on each level, usually away from the active digging to minimize their exposure to dust and noise.

Once hauled to the surface, the ore was crushed into smaller pieces at stamping mills. Furnaces smelted the crushed rock to separate the copper from the limestone rock. It was further refined after shipping it to nearby railheads.

Crypto Scene

The Mule Mountains surround Bisbee. While few people pay close attention to the ground they walk on, the geology of any given area forecasts its future in many unforeseen ways. For the casual observer with an untrained eye, the Mule Mountains may reveal little of the riches that lie beneath our

One by one, helmet lights wink on to light the darkness ahead as visitors ride an original Trolley Motor single-file into the Queen Mine to begin their exploration.

footsteps. In fact, the ground may seem dull and unappealing. However, the geologic process that started here long before dinosaurs roamed the Earth set the stage for the human dramas that followed.

The first crucial steps in the history of copper in the region began during the Age of Fishes, the Paleozoic era, from 500 million to 240 million year ago. Covered by vast oceans, the Southwest witnessed the formation of limestone. The host rock for the copper deposits at the Queen Mine is limestone. Limestone belongs to one of three large classifications of rock called *sedimentary* (the other two are *igneous* and *metamorphic*). Formed by the gradual accumulation of the shells of tiny living creatures such as snails, clams, and foraminifera, or the gradual chemical precipitation of lime from fresh or seawater, limestone is relatively soft rock that can be scratched with the blade of a knife. A small drop of dilute hydrochloric acid on the surface of limestone will cause it to effervesce. This sensitivity to mild acids creates small cavities or *vugs* and fissures in the limestone, thanks to the acids from rainwater and groundwater. The vugs become pockets that collect precious minerals and gemstones.

Subjected to heat from volcanic magma forced up from deep within the Earth, hot solutions containing minerals—including copper, lead, zinc, silver, and even gold—filled the crevices and fissures in the limestone. While sounding simple, the mineralization process occurred over 70 million years, starting at a time when dinosaurs roamed the regions to the north. The deposits of the dissolved minerals were different each time, frequently containing different amounts of copper, lead, and other minerals. Over time, the result was a rich deposit of minerals ready and waiting for discovery. History would later reveal that in less than 100 years, between 1877 and 1975, the geology around Bisbee would produce 8 billion pounds of copper, 355 million pounds of zinc, 324 million pounds of lead, 100 million ounces of silver, and 8 million ounces of gold.

Miners used this portable latrine car while they were deep underground. It was not very private and more than likely a little smelly, too!

Own a Piece of the Rock

Take the time to visit the museum at the Queen Mine or one of several rock shops in Bisbee to see samples of bright blue azurite and green malachite found in limestone vugs and in close association with copper ore. Both minerals are ideal pieces for a personal rock collection. An excellent little mineral shop on Brewery Gulch Road has convenient starter collections that include several types of minerals attached to a card with identification labels. Each fall, Bisbee hosts a gem and mineral show, and of course, Tucson features a very large annual show.

Micro Scape

Can you identify how minerals play an important role in our lives? Every American uses about 1,925 pounds of copper during his or her lifetime. What are some of the uses of copper that come to your mind? To start with, the penny in your pocket is coated with copper. Did you know that about 40 different minerals are needed to manufacture a computer? Did you know that copper is used in electrical motors and in most household appliances (such as refrigerators)? Did you think to include the wiring in your house that brings electricity to the wall socket and the light switch? In regions subjected to electrical storms, lightning rods rely on copper wire to direct the energy from a bolt of lightning to the ground.

Defined as a natural, homogeneous, non-living solid with a crystalline atomic structure, each mineral has a chemical formula. For pure copper, the chemical symbol is Cu. It is hard to imagine living without copper and other minerals from the earth. Our society has become dependent on minerals, yet sometimes we forget where they come from. Without minerals, our way of life would be significantly different.

Our society's thirst for copper during the Age of Electricity fueled the growth of the mining industry. The heyday of the Queen Mine ran a parallel course to the evolution of inventions such as the electric lightbulb, telegraph,

Inside one of the tunnels, miners-turned-tour-guides lend a first-hand perspective to the history of early mining techniques and the hazards of being a miner.

telephone, and phonograph—all, to one degree or another, dependent on copper and other minerals.

Puerta de las Mulas (Mule Pass) was a reliable trail used by the Apache Indians as early as 1848 when returning from raids on *ranchos* in Mexico. Gradually, others started using the pass, including soldiers, explorers, and settlers to the area. Today, a tunnel carved through the pass carries traffic on AZ 80 into Bisbee.

As with much of the West, the military and its scouts stationed on the frontier unlocked the secrets of this unfamiliar territory. A civilian tracker and part-time prospector by the name of Jack Dunn is credited with the discovery of the potential mineral wealth of the Mule Mountains and the area that later became the town of Bisbee. Dunn, along with a group of soldiers from nearby Fort Bowie, was trying to capture Indian renegades. The group camped for the night very close to what is now downtown Bisbee. The next morning, they located better water at a rock formation called Castle Rock, which stands today across the street from the Castle Rock Inn on Main Street.

Marching up the hillside, the town of Bisbee has evolved from a raw frontier mining town to a collection of art galleries, antique stores, restaurants, and gem and fine jewelry shops, complete with Victorian-era ambiance. Tours of the Bisbee Mining and Historic Museum, St. Patrick's Catholic Church, and the Art Deco county courthouse collectively paint a vivid picture of Bisbee's history. The town hosts several annual events, including the 1,000 Stair Climb and a historic home tour.

While exploring the area, Dunn found a mineral associated with silver and quickly grasped the potential of his discovery.

In August 1877, Dunn filed a claim on the land. Unfortunately for Dunn, he shared the information with a shady business partner, George Warren, who robbed Dunn of his place in history as "The Father of the Camp," or Bisbee. Not only was Dunn robbed of his fame, but heavy drinking habits and gambling left Warren penniless at his death. A large white tombstone marks the grave of George Warren in the Evergreen cemetery in Bisbee.

Riches from the Earth Build a Town

The town of Bisbee owes its existence to copper and other minerals extracted from the Earth. Walking the streets today, visitors catch an occasional glimpse into its past through the remaining buildings and other clues that reflect its heyday. The Copper Queen Hotel on Howell Street, in the center of Bisbee, is the longest continuously operated hotel in Arizona. Brewery Gulch was once the most notorious street in Bisbee. It hosted more than 40 saloons at one time, and because it was in a wash, it frequently suffered from flash floods. Early mining techniques and building construction removed almost all the trees from the hillsides, so when it rained there was nothing to hold the soil in place or soak up the water. Even the lightest rain caused massive flooding. Citizens could do little to stop the floods. According to humorous stories, shopkeepers opened the front and back doors and let the raging waters just pass right through.

 Travel Log

- Queen Mine contact information: cityofbisbee.com/queenminetours, 520-432-2071, 866-432-2071.

- Queen Mine is located in Bisbee, about 100 miles southeast of Tucson. Take I-10 east to AZ 80 south.

- The Queen Mine Underground Tour is open seven days a week, year-round, closing only for Thanksgiving Day and Dec. 25. Call 520-432-2071 or 1-866-432-2071 for information. Reservations are recommended.

- Bisbee offers a variety of shops, art galleries, and many restored buildings that offer several alternatives for lunch or dinner.

- Several old boarding houses from the mining era have been restored and live again as bed-and-breakfast facilities, should you decide to extend your stay.

- The town has evolved into an artists' colony featuring an odd assortment of Victorian-era charm and more avant-garde touches, offering both historic and artistic experiences.

- Take a light jacket, comfortable walking shoes, and a camera with a flash.

- For your rock collection: Look for azurite and malachite.

14 Saguaro National Park

The landscape of Saguaro National Park seems to be populated by gigantic human forms. Most stand exceptionally tall and slender. Some possess peering eyes from which woodpeckers peek. Others appear to hold beautiful bouquets of white flowers in their curving arms.

"We call him our brother, and we know that he was put at this place for a very special reason," explains an American Indian named Daniel Preston. "We want to have that strong image and that tall image about ourselves as people. So, when we look at the saguaro, we begin to try to acquire those qualities." Preston offers this perspective of his Tohono O'odham people to visitors enjoying the cool darkness of the theater at Red Hills Visitor Center in Saguaro National Park's Tucson Mountain District.

A refreshing place to escape the desert sun and enjoy a colorful slide show, the automated auditorium presents more than just basic information. It offers inspiration. "This desert can speak to each of us in many ways," concludes the narrator. The screen begins to rise and wide curtains open slowly to reveal a grand view of the dense saguaro forest outside. The surprising effect is unforgettable, leaving visitors wanting to see and learn more about this stunning landscape.

West Side, East Side

Although the west district of the park is closer to downtown Tucson and smaller than the east district, the cactus-studded hillsides offer plenty of opportunities to become familiar with the giant saguaro.

Listening is a good way to get to know this desert community. Take a peaceful morning stroll on the 0.5-mile Desert Discovery Trail off Kinney Road to hear the Sonoran Desert soundscape as it awakes with the calls of Gila woodpeckers and coos of white-winged doves. Walk quietly on the easy, winding trail and you will encounter a surprise around every corner. A startling flash of black and white serves up a warning sign as a zebratail lizard curls its striped tail and shuffles off into the dry brush. Squeaks and chirps arise from a hidden nest as a gilded flicker darts from the cavity in a cactus trunk. Up high on the skeletal top of a broken saguaro, a collared lizard bounces and bobs before descending into the hollow refuge of the dead cactus.

Saguaros, the largest cacti in the United States, grow only in the Sonoran Desert.
Special water-saving adaptations enable saguaros to survive in this dry climate,
where they may reach a height of 50 feet and live more than 150 years.

Colorful wayside signs along the Freeman Homestead Trail feature a children's corner with artwork drawn by local school children. Each panel challenges hikers to test their skills at living in and learning from the desert environment.

The skeletal image of a dying saguaro offers a glimpse of the strong support system that allows this cactus to reach great heights and bear more than 6 tons in weight. Beneath the prickly spines and waxy skin protecting the cactus from evaporation, spongy flesh that stores water surrounds the interconnected wooden ribs. Local people once used saguaro ribs to construct the walls of homes, or as poles to pick the fruits of the saguaro.

Beyond a few bends in the trail, a multiarmed saguaro cactus reaches down to the ground, creating a fort for anyone short, before a faint rustle alerts you to another desert dweller nearby. Something sluggish lumbers off its perch on a nearby log. Maybe it is a seldom-seen Gila monster or a roadrunner trying to corner its prey.

East of Tucson, the Freeman Homestead Trail in the Rincon Mountain District offers another unhurried experience as well as a chance to learn from other young explorers along the way. Rugged rock steps lead hikers through a natural garden of creosote, saguaros, and scattered ocotillos where colorful interpretive signs include activities for children. The children's corner on each wayside panel features artwork drawn by local kids in fourth through sixth grade who have hiked the 1-mile loop trail on school outings. Some panels include brainteasers that challenge hikers to find the remnants of an ocotillo fence at the site of an old adobe homestead or to identify an animal that may have nibbled on a nearby cactus. One sign even instructs hikers on how to check for water in the sand of a hot, dry wash! Discovering such interesting facts makes this a fun hike for everyone.

Bicycling, backcountry hiking, or horseback riding are other ways to encounter the astounding variety of the park, but careful planning and plenty of time are necessary. Few people ever experience the 100-square-mile backcountry, which features environments ranging from grassy foothills to pine woodlands. So much wilderness—70,000 acres—so close to the city make the Rincon Mountains of Saguaro National Park's west district a good place for a getaway without being too far from civilization.

Crypto Scene

Underground, a saguaro cactus is as wide as it is tall! Just a few inches below the surface, a maze of shallow roots spreads out as far as the height of the plant to collect valuable water during infrequent rains. Such a reservoir system can gather 200 gallons of water from a single rainfall. Supported by a skeleton of strong, woody ribs, an adult six-ton saguaro can stockpile one ton of water. Where does all that moisture go? The vertical pleats of the saguaro expand like an accordion, allowing the spongy flesh beneath to store water as a jelly-like substance. In drier months, the pleats shrink as the plant survives on moisture absorbed during the brief spring and monsoon showers.

Wild Things

When you think of the desert, you probably do not picture the Mexican long-tongued and lesser long-nosed bats so important to the pollination of saguaro flowers. Jowly javelinas preying on prickly pears probably do not come to mind, either. A more common symbol of this arid landscape is the desert tortoise, a reptile that lives underground most of the time, emerging now and then for water, grass, flowers, and fruit.

To learn more about desert tortoises, researchers attach small radios to the shells of some animals to track their movements. Although tortoises usually stay within a home area of only a few hundred yards, one tortoise nicknamed Thelma walked 20 miles away from the east side of Saguaro National Park! Thelma was spotted on private property, along railroad tracks, and even walking on the shoulder of I-10. When a concerned citizen called to report her whereabouts—to prevent her from being run over or picked up illegally to become a pet—researchers returned Thelma to the national park where she had first been released. As far as scientists know, Thelma stayed in the park, where more than 135 adult tortoises live in each square mile.

Micro Scape

Seedling saguaros rely on larger plants to become established in the dry desert. Shade from "nurse trees" such as mesquite, ironwood, or palo verde, protects tiny saguaros, which grow less than 2 inches in their first eight years! Hike for a while on a hot, sunny day in the desert and you will certainly understand the importance of shade. Upon first glance, no relief may be in sight. Look harder and you will realize that you can stand in the shadow of

Saguaros provide shelter for many wildlife species. This mourning dove mother and nestling rest on the burly arm of a spiny giant.

the narrowest saguaro and find some shelter from the sun. Look even harder and you will discover that even giant saguaros find shade in the desert. In fact, they make their own! Groups of sharp spines not only protect the fleshy cactus from gnawing javelinas, woodrats, and rabbits, they also cast splotchy shadows on the surface of the plant. Examine the spines on a small saguaro cactus, and you will see that this resourceful plant is growing in its own shade. Spines also help the saguaro survive—often to 200 years—by forming a sort of windbreak against dry, desert breezes.

Back in Time Line

Bats, birds, insects, rodents, and coyotes are not the only desert dwellers that depend on saguaros for food and shelter. Almost 2,000 years ago, the Hohokam people relied on native plants the way we rely on supermarkets today. Although seasonal rains allowed them to grow squash, corn, and beans, they also survived by hunting deer, rabbits, and other small animals,

In spring, saguaros produce showy white flowers each night for about a month. Flying pollinators such as bats, birds, and insects feed the nectar, and the flowers wilt away by the next afternoon. Bright red fruits appear in summer; each contains as many as 2,000 seeds, which are eaten and dispersed by wildlife.

and by gathering plants such as prickly pear cactus, cholla, mesquite beans, agave, and saguaro fruit. Saguaros bloom in May or June and produce red, juicy, fig-like fruit into July. During this hot, dry season, the Hohokam would use the strong wooden ribs of the saguaro, which they tied together with a crosspiece at the top, to harvest the ripe fruit from high on the cactus branches. Each fruit, filled with as many as 2,000 tiny black seeds, could be savored immediately or dried and eaten when other foods were scarce. Although drought or poor soil conditions may have led to the disappearance of the Hohokam people (whose name is sometimes translated as "all used up") around the year 1450, their ties to the saguaro were maintained by the Tohono O'odham people, who may be their descendants.

Today, the Tohono O'odham carry on the traditions of desert living established so long ago. These "people of the desert" still build shelters and fences with saguaro ribs and collect the pulpy red fruits using saguaro poles. Even though they shop at modern markets, they still make saguaro jelly, candy, and a wine used in a ceremony to trigger the summer rains. Wasting nothing, the Tohono O'odham even use the seeds as chicken feed.

Travel Log

- Saguaro National Park contact information: nps.gov/sagu, 520-733-5100.

- Saguaro National Park consists of two areas divided by the city of Tucson: the Tucson Mountain District on the west and the Rincon Mountain District 30 miles to the east.

- To reach Saguaro West from I-10, take the Speedway Boulevard exit (257), and travel 13 miles west on Gates Pass Road. This route is very narrow and winding in some places, so drive carefully and be prepared to share the road with bicyclists. Continue northwest on Kinney Road 10 miles to the Red Hills Visitor Center.

- To reach Saguaro East from I-10, take the Houghton Road exit (275), and travel 7.8 miles north to East Escalante Road. Continue 2 miles east to South Old Spanish Trail and the park entrance. Both districts are literally at the doorstep of Tucson, where restaurants, fuel stations, and other services abound.

- Safety in this hot desert climate is very, very important. From May through September, midday temperatures can average in the 100s. Shade is scarce, so explore the park in the cooler early morning hours, apply sunscreen, wear a hat, and take plenty of water on any stroll or hike (a gallon per person per day is recommended). From October through April, high temperatures reach into the 60s and 70s.

- Try not to touch chollas, prickly pears, saguaros, and other desert plants whose spines may lead to painful encounters.

Desert tortoises survive with natural camouflage that helps them look like rocks, blending into the landscape. Researchers can study desert tortoise behavior using telemetry, receiving signals from a small radio attached to the tortoise's shell.

photo courtesy of Jim Rorabaugh

- Only 12 inches of rain may fall in an entire year, but if a thunderstorm occurs during your visit, avoid flash floods and lightning by seeking shelter in your vehicle or at the visitor center. Avoid open and low-lying areas. Poisonous animals such as rattlesnakes, scorpions, and Gila monsters usually avoid humans, but be aware of their presence; keep your hands and feet away from rock crevices or other hidden places where you may surprise one of these desert dwellers.

- Bring binoculars, a camera, and a hand lens to enjoy learning about the lush Sonoran Desert. Saguaro National Park offers a free self-guided junior ranger program that features a choice of activity booklets and a discovery pack for checkout, which includes supplies for completing the activities. Junior ranger day camp programs are also available (for a small fee) and include activities such as hikes, craft projects, petroglyph making, and games. Ranger-guided field trips and outreach programs for students of all ages are also available.

- Saguaro National Park is open daily throughout the year.

- For your rock collection: The national park lies at the foot of the Rincon Mountains; a specific type of schist (a metamorphic rock) called phyllite is associated with this range.

15

Tumacácori National Historical Park

Smoke from a small fire puffs across the patio as a woman makes fresh tortillas in the shade of a ramada. Try one of these traditional treats as you start off on the trail at Mission San José de Tumacácori, and experience a taste of the rich history of a region that has witnessed conflict and conquest as well as peace and prosperity. (*Tumacácori* is O'odham for a "flat, rocky place.") More than 300 years of footsteps have fallen this way since Spanish explorers first encountered tribes here along the Santa Cruz River. Notice the foundations that remain of the homes of the native O'odham people and trace their tracks through time as you approach the impressive church ruins.

In the early 1800s, these grounds bustled with church-building commotion as workers manufactured adobe bricks from the red soil. High above in the sturdy but unfinished arched tower, tolling bells announced the end of a workday just as crews returned from a long journey in the mountains to find timbers for the roof. Detailed columns and fragments of bright paint continue to accent the massive adobe walls, although nothing but lizards now live where workers once prepared mortar and limestone plaster, anticipating the holy masses and ceremonies to come.

Mission Accomplished

Pass through the enormous church entrance and feel the cool quiet that greeted Indians and Spanish settlers kneeling side by side to hear a Franciscan priest sing mass in Latin. Joined by a choir positioned in the loft, his voice would echo off the high ceilings as if sent from heaven. Dressed in colorful vestments, the priest offered prayers while surrounded by ornate artwork that remains in the sanctuary today. Wander from room to room to examine the 9-foot-thick walls of the baptistry and the dark sacristy that priests used to store clothing, important records, and other items. Even now, in its declined state, it's easy to visualize masses, marriages, baptisms, and funerals taking place in this grand piece of architecture. If you visit in October, you can make an advance reservation to attend a historic High Mass, or *Misa Major,* inside

Enter the old church ruins at Tumacácori and you are transported back to when Spanish missions punctuated the region. Original plans for the church included a dome on the bell tower (right), but a lack of funds prevented its construction.

the church. Dressed in traditional costumes, a choir with musicians and a local priest take part. All participants, young and old, are expected to wear Spanish or American Indian clothing to recreate an authentic experience from the 18th and 19th centuries.

Outside the church to the north lies the cemetery with its unusual circular mortuary, another unfinished element of the mission. Although few markers exist, this is considered holy ground. More than 600 dead were buried here, mostly between 1755 and 1825. Remnants of this early era remain just east of the church, where the foundation of another adobe building lingers in the dust. When Jesuit Father Eusebio Kino first arrived at the O'odham village here in 1691, he stopped on the opposite side of the Santa Cruz River to celebrate mass for the villagers under a brush ramada. Kino soon built a mission at a place called Guevavi to the south. However, in 1695, he constructed a small house at Tumacácori, which he used as a church on his return visits. It was not until 1753 that construction of an official church began at this spot, where only a foundation exists today. Jesuit priests conducted services here until 1767, when they were forced to return to Europe. Franciscan priests carried on their work in the building until 1822, when services could be held in the new church you see today. To the south, you can see ruins of the priests' quarters, or *convento*.

If you'd like to see how the interior of the church at Tumacácori National Historical Park may have appeared in the early 1800s, venture north to Mission San Xavier del Bac near Tucson. Known as the "White Dove of the Desert," Mission San Xavier del Bac was built in the late 1700s and is still used as a parish church today. It has been beautifully restored with gilded statues and elaborate paintings.

Continue exploring the mission grounds to discover more about life along the Santa Cruz River. Once you have walked the paths of Father Kino, the Jesuit and Franciscan priests who followed him, and the O'odham, Apache, and other native people who set foot on Tumacácori soil, you will get hooked on Arizona history. You, yourself, will become a link in a cultural corridor stretching from Sonora, Mexico, to Tucson and beyond.

Crypto Scene

Tumacácori National Historical Park includes two additional missions: Guevavi (O'odham for "big water") and Calabazas. Located south of Tumacácori and east of the river, both sites contain only ruined traces of mission structures built in the mid-1700s. Guevavi remains of particular importance, though, as the oldest mission in Arizona and the location of the mission headquarters established by Father Kino in 1691. Kino would pass through Guevavi on horseback as he traveled from the mission at Dolores, Mexico, and north to Tumacácori and San Xavier del Bac near present-day Tucson. Years of hardship, including disease and American Indian revolts, prompted the relocation of mission headquarters to Tumacácori in 1771. The public can visit Guevavi and Calabazas only by special arrangement with the National Park Service.

Wild Things

Enjoy a short walk on the Juan de Bautista de Anza National Historic Trail along the banks of the Santa Cruz River where the rich streamside, or *riparian*, environment supports a fascinating variety of plants and animals. This cottonwood/willow ecosystem provides habitat for nearly every type of resident wildlife, including more than 200 bird species such as Western tanagers, vermilion flycatchers, gray hawks, and the elusive yellow-billed cuckoo, a robin-size relative of the roadrunner.

Just northeast of Tumacácori, the riparian area provides habitat for a concentration of breeding yellow-billed cuckoos. Gray, with a patterned black-and-white tail, cuckoos have curved bills that are yellow on the bottom. Cuckoos build twig nests in the cottonwoods, where they feed on large insects such as cicadas and caterpillars as well as lizards and frogs.

What is so important about these cuckoos? Such birds may be indicators of healthy riparian ecosystems. Yellow-billed cuckoos breed from southern Canada south into Mexico. Although they are common east of the Continental Divide, populations have been declining rapidly throughout the West. Researchers estimate that invading weeds, pesticide use, agriculture, dams, overgrazing, and development have caused the loss of more than 90 percent of the bird's riparian habitat. Here at Tumacácori, amid what seems to be a

Mexican dancers at La Fiesta de Tumacácori thrill onlookers with their expert moves and brightly colored costumes. Photo courtesy of National Park Service

never-ending cottonwood grove, the yellow-billed cuckoo is still able to find refuge from the effects of most human interference.

Micro Scape

Retreat to the shade of the Tumacácori garden and you will experience many of the same sights and sounds enjoyed in mission courtyards hundreds of years ago. A trickling fountain offers a chance for reflection. The fragrance of sage and rosemary wafts through the air and pepper, pomegranate, olive, and apricot trees create an oasis where roses and other flowers flourish. Thrashers and wrens make ratchety noises as they dart in and out, searching for seeds and bugs.

Although this courtyard was not constructed until 1937 when the National Park Service built the Tumacácori visitor center, it is a realistic recreation of a peaceful mission garden. Trees, shrubs, and herbs typical of Spanish missions throughout the West were included, along with Sonoran Desert species, so visitors can appreciate the value of plants in mission life. Mission courtyards of 300 years ago were also important areas for growing fruits and vegetables as well as for growing ornamental species simply for their beauty. Investigate the plantings along the curved garden path and try to identify familiar fruits or flowers. Which plants may have been used for medicine or as fiber for clothing in the past?

After Spanish conquistadors such as Coronado traveled into this region and intruded on lands occupied by native people, there were still no settlers to civilize what was called "New Spain." As a result, the Spanish mission system was established to convert natives to Christianity and make them taxpayers loyal to the Spanish Crown. In this effort, mission priests educated tribes such as the O'odham and gave them food and clothing.

In 1687, an Italian Jesuit priest named Father Eusebio Francisco Kino enthusiastically brought the Catholic faith to the Santa Cruz Valley. Riding horseback while dressed in a black robe, he tirelessly explored 50,000 square miles of the Pimería Alta (now northern Mexico and southern Arizona). Father Kino was welcomed for his eagerness to understand local cultures and his generosity and genuine concern for the native people. In 1691, he and another priest visited the ranchería of Tumacácori, held mass, performed baptisms, and moved on to do the same at Guevavi. Both places became missions in a cluster managed by Father Kino from his first mission, Nuestra Senora de los Dolores (better known as Mission Dolores), established in Sonora, Mexico, in 1687.

During his 24 years in the Pimería Alta, Kino introduced cattle and sheep as well as the cultivation of wheat and fruit trees to the villagers, who primarily grew corn, squash, and beans. Known today as the "padre on

Historical demonstrations on the mission grounds include traditional tortilla making under the shade of a wooden ramada.

horseback," Father Kino constantly explored the Sonoran Desert, studying the stars and mapping new lands while fulfilling his missionary duties. When many still thought California was an island, a gift of blue shells given to him by the Yumas prompted Father Kino to find their source and prove that a land connection existed to the Sonoran Desert. His good relationships with people throughout the region joined them together to survive repeated Apache raids, while his peacekeeping abilities helped end a local conflict in 1695. By the time Father Kino died in 1711 at the age of 73, he had become one of the West's most admired figures, founding 27 missions from the Rio Sonora in Mexico to the Santa Catalina Mountains near present-day Tucson.

Cultural Crossroads

An uprising against Spanish settlements in 1751 led to the establishment of a military post, or *presidio,* just north of Tumacácori at Tubac. When the Spanish Crown removed the Jesuit priests from New Spain because of a power struggle, they were replaced by the gray-robed Franciscans, whose artful mission architecture surpassed the simple building techniques of the Jesuits. Spanish soldiers from the presidio, such as Captain Juan Bautista de Anza, maintained order in the colonies while the Franciscans tended to the spiritual needs of the people. Although Captain Anza's duties were mainly military, he was able to pursue his goal of linking the Pimería Alta to California. In 1774, he led an exploration that established a trail for a more elaborate expedition one year later. In 1775-1776, an entire colony of Sonorans followed the route to create a community at San Francisco Bay.

Established by Father Eusebio Francisco Kino in 1692, Mission San Xavier del Bac is located 10 miles north of Tumacácori National Historical Park, where it continues to serve as an active mission. Those who view the rustic remains of the church at Tumacácori are awestruck by the ornate interior of San Xavier, known as the greatest example of Spanish colonial architecture in the United States.

Although military operations relocated to Tucson in 1776, Franciscan friars continued to build elaborate churches at places such as Tumacácori and San Xavier del Bac, where meager adobes once stood. Construction slowed and support from Spain dwindled, however, between 1810 and 1821 during the Mexican War of Independence. The beautiful church at Tumacácori was nearly finished when all the Spanish priests were forced from the region in 1828. With Apache raids on the rise and settlers departing, Mexican priests became unable to maintain the church. By 1948, Tubac and Tumacácori had become abandoned casualties of cultural conflict.

Travel Log

- Tumacácori National Historical Park contact information: nps.gov/tuma, 520-398-2341.

- To reach Tumacácori National Historical Park, drive 45 miles south from Tucson on I-19 to exit 29, and follow the signs.

- The park is located 18 miles north of the Mexican border at Nogales, Arizona, and is open daily from 8 a.m. to 5 p.m., except on Thanksgiving Day and Dec. 25.

- Kids will enjoy an innovative junior ranger program, including an activity that involves historical costumes of Jesuit and Franciscan priests, O'odham, Apache, and Spanish people.

- A self-guided interpretive booklet is available, and guided tours of the mission church and grounds are provided by rangers and docents during the winter months. Historical craft demonstrations such as basket weaving, tortilla making, or Mexican pottery making take place most weekends September through June. Plan on a half-day to explore the mission grounds and enjoy the museum exhibits.

- During winter, rangers conduct guided tours of Missions Calabazas and Guevavi each Wednesday. A non-refundable fee is required and reservations must be made by calling 520-398-2341, extension 0.

- An enjoyable full-day excursion includes Tubac Presidio State Historic Park (just north of Tumacácori) and Mission San Xavier del Bac (10 miles south of Tucson on I-19 at exit 92).

- Attend La Fiesta de Tumacácori on the first weekend of December from 10 a.m. to 5 p.m. to experience samples of traditional American Indian, Mexican, and Southwestern cultures. Food and crafts are featured along with live stage performances and special activities for children. Sunday events include a mariachi procession and a mass in front of the old mission church. During Tubac's Anza Days, attendance at High Mass inside the church at Tumacácori is limited and advance reservations are required. For reservations, call 520-398-2341.

16

Verde Valley

Descend into the Verde Valley in summer and you will agree that *verde* (Spanish for "green") remains the best word to describe this basin, no matter how hot and dry the surrounding landscape. Although the valley was actually named for a green copper mineral, the water that flows year-round in the meandering river and creeks below is responsible for the area's emerald hue.

"The river is known to never have gone dry," says the narrator on the Verde Canyon Railroad. A 40-mile round-trip excursion on this scenic railway hugs the Verde River all the way from Clarkdale to Perkinsville and back, slowly rolling along past limestone cliffs and views of Black Mountain in the distance. "Back in the saddle again, back where a friend is a friend," is heard throughout the railcars as the cowboy poet narrator adds song and guitar music to his story of Verde Canyon. Passengers join in, swaying along, singing the song, trying to stay steady on their feet or in their seats.

As the locomotive heads toward the mouth of the canyon, creaking along on the highest and longest trestle on the trip, the view of the snaking river 150 feet below is memorable. Interesting tales of American Indians and pioneers can be heard over the speakers while passengers settle down to enjoy snacks, beverages, or even a game of cards. Outside the panoramic views feature remarkable geological formations, including outcroppings shaped like an elephant and a turtle. Lush groves of sycamore, walnut, and cottonwood trees contrast with colorful red sandstone cliffs, enticing passengers to photo-graph the scene from the breezy, open-air cars. Out in the open, everyone gets a thrill as the train passes through a dark, 680-foot tunnel with limestone walls only 6 inches away in some spots!

Emerging from Verde Canyon, wide meadows appear where Perkinsville marks the turnaround point for the engine. According to the lively narrator, this site of a railroad station built in 1912 is "not just a one-horse town, it's a one-house town!" Once populated by about a dozen families, Perkinsville seems like a ghost town now, except for a single ranch with some livestock. A startled horse snorts and trots away when the loud horn blows to alert all that the engine will soon pass on a siding. Brightly painted with the face of a bald eagle, the engine hooks onto the opposite end of the train and the return trip to the depot begins. Just when you think you can set down your

Passengers are treated to inspiring views of towering cliffs and lush streamside vegetation on a 40-mile round-trip excursion on the Verde Canyon Railroad from Clarkdale to Perkinsville.
photo courtesy of Verde Canyon Railroad

camera, the railroad's mascot makes a surprise appearance in the brilliant blue sky. A majestic bald eagle soars high above the river as if to suggest there is always more to see in the Verde Canyon.

On the way back to Clarkdale, the cowboy narrator strolls through the railcars, sharing tunes and poems that confirm how much more there is to experience in the Verde Valley.

Footprints in Time

The smell of the leather, the dew in the morn, the campfire's a burnin', just trying to keep warm. The coffee's a boilin', the biscuits rise high, my mount's gettin' restless; he's ready to ride.

An Arizona sunrise is beckonin' me, to ride across the plains, a lot of beauty to see. Cactus and canyons, where rivers run free, Arizona's building memories for me.

An old Sinaguan dwelling's tucked under a ledge; it's a playground for lizards, where potshards are spread. An old packrat is building a home, where the wind blows lonely, Sinaguans once roamed.

Many footprints have been left, in this desolate land, but they've now disappeared, in the shifting dry sands, maybe to appear on another windy day, showing this old cowhand, once passed this way.

Wil Adams, The Arizona Cowboy Balladeer and Poet

Paleo Scene

The chalky gray limestone of the Verde Valley is bordered on the northeast by the Mogollon Rim and on the southwest by the Central Highlands. North of the Verde Valley, the Colorado Plateau features cooler temperatures and dense forests. An abrupt change is obvious where the sedimentary rock of the plateau has eroded to form the 2,000-foot-high backbone that separates much of northern Arizona from the southern part of the state. Elevations atop the Mogollon Rim average between 6,500 and 7,000 feet. At the base of the rim, where warmer and drier conditions exist, elevations range from 4,000 to 4,500 feet.

South of Verde Valley, the Verde Fault is easy to recognize, especially as you ascend US 89A from Clarkdale to the historic mining town of Jerome. Although Spanish explorers may have discovered gold here in 1583, Jerome's real riches came in the form of copper ore. Area mines produced more than $375 million in copper—along with silver, gold, and zinc—between 1876 and 1953. Positioned on steep terrain between two branches of the fault, the town of Jerome actually shifted downhill when blasting in the mines created shocks as strong as an earthquake!

Birdwatchers can see bald eagles just about anytime in Verde Canyon, where a population of these majestic birds resides year-round. However, the best time to look for eagles in the canyon is during the winter migration of bald and golden eagles. During the months of December through March, more than 30 eagles can be seen skimming the river for fish or perched on cottonwoods, basking in the sun.

photo courtesy of Jim Rorabaugh

Wild Things

Yellow-beaked with white heads and brown bodies, bald eagles can have wingspans of up to 7 feet, making them a spectacular sight along the Verde River. In summer, passengers on the Verde Canyon Railroad are particularly surprised to see bald eagles perched on a nest of sticks or skimming across the shallow water to catch a trout. Wildlife watchers expect to see more than 30 bald and golden eagles here in winter when many migratory birds flock to Arizona for its warm temperatures. In Verde Canyon, however, bald eagles can be observed year-round!

Bald eagles in Arizona breed earlier in the year than eagles in other locations. Adults lay eggs from December to March and the eggs hatch in about 35 days. In May and June, 12-week-old eaglets leave their nests. The young generally migrate north after 45 days. In Arizona and Mexico, 36 breeding pairs of bald eagles do not migrate. These eagles make up a unique population of year-round residents. One such pair of bald eagles continuously nests on the steep volcanic cliffs of the Verde River where they have lived for more than 10 years. Eagles usually mate for life—in fact, this couple has produced at least seven young since 1993, making Verde Canyon one of the best birding destinations in the state.

Multicolored cliffs guard the Verde River along its snaking course toward Clarkdale. Verde Canyon contains American Indian dwellings, a variety of wildlife, and evidence of early pioneer and mining history.

photo courtesy of Verde Canyon Railroad

Look for a hilltop covered with lumpy rocks between the farming and ranching communities of Cottonwood and Clarkdale. From about 1,000 to 600 years ago, people lived there in a two-story village made of stone walls perched 120 feet above the verdant river valley. Today, the remnants of this ancient community are preserved as Tuzigoot National Monument (*Tuzigoot* is Apache for "crooked water").

Known as the Sinaguan people, this Pueblo culture occupied the Verde Valley for the same reasons people do today: year-round water for agriculture and moderate temperatures. Walk along the Ruins Loop Trail to imagine life in this prehistoric community. Builders would have hauled heavy limestone and sandstone blocks up from the valley floor to build foundations for nearly a hundred small rooms. Mud and clay brought up from the river were used as mortar and plaster for the dwellings. Cottonwood, sycamore, and juniper branches were carried up the steep trail to make rafters for the roofs. On a hot day, you can appreciate the labor of the Sinaguan architects as you rest in the coolness of a reconstructed room at the top of the trail.

The Verde Valley Sinaguans adopted an irrigation system established earlier by the Hohokam culture and successfully grew cotton, squash, and

The Ruins Loop Trail at Tuzigoot National Monument leads to the reconstructed dwellings of the Sinagua, an early Pueblo culture of the Verde Valley. Mesquite, along with cottonwood and sycamore groves, line the banks of the Verde River.

corn to supplement the walnuts, grapes, mesquite beans, rabbit, duck, elk, and other native plants and animals found in the valley. Weavers used the cotton to make blankets and sashes, while yucca and beargrass were used in nets, cloth, and baskets. Visit the Sinaguan Room exhibit in the Tuzigoot Visitor Center to understand how skilled these people were at making tools, garments and baskets. Also on display is an excellent collection of artifacts ranging from beautifully crafted jewelry to trade goods such as shells and turquoise. In the early 1400s, the Sinaguans abandoned the Verde Valley, possibly because of conflicts with the Yavapais or because of too much pressure on area resources. They probably moved north to join other Pueblo communities, leaving the valley to be occupied by a succession of American Indians, Spanish explorers, military troops, settlers, and farmers.

In 1883, copper mining gave rise to the town of Jerome in the Black Hills above the Verde Valley. Open-pit mines necessitated a smelter, so Clarkdale was built at a lower elevation where ore from Jerome could be crushed, cooked, and cast into copper bars. Unfortunately, sulphur-laden smoke killed grass and trees in nearby orchards, and mine tailings choked the valley. Although mining ceased here more than 50 years ago, you can still see waste from the smelter operation when you visit the national monument. Today, Tuzigoot's Tavasci Marsh is undergoing restoration to provide the clean water and healthy wildlife habitat the Sinaguans must have known, while the life-giving waters of the Verde River continue to nourish Verde Valley farms and ranches.

Travel Log

- Verde Valley and Tuzigoot National Monument contact information: nps.gov/tuzi, 928-634-5564.

- To reach Tuzigoot National Monument, take I-17 north from Phoenix or south from Flagstaff to exit 287 and follow US 260 west to Cottonwood. In Cottonwood, take Main Street north toward Clarkdale. A sign directs you to the monument entrance. Tuzigoot is 52 miles south of Flagstaff and 90 miles north of Phoenix.

- The monument is open daily from 8 a.m. to 5 p.m. (6 p.m. in summer), but closed on Dec. 25. Call 928-634-5564 for further information.

- From Clarkdale, continue to a fork in the road where a sign points right toward the Verde Canyon Railroad. Veer right onto North Broadway to the train depot.

- Call 1-800-293-7245 for rates and information on seasonal highlights such as the January eagle watch and the fall color tour in October and November. Special holiday train rides include the Easter Bunny Express, Haunted Halloween Express, and the Santa Claus Express.

- For your rock collection: Two copper minerals are important in the early mining history of the valley—malachite and the rarer chalcopyrite.

17 Walnut Canyon National Monument

Discovery Zone

Dad calls out, "Save your energy! You have 240 steps to get back out of the canyon!" Probably a good thing to keep in mind, descending the limestone steps into Walnut Canyon and the Island Trail, although a delightful discovery waits ahead. Prehistoric Sinagua (Spanish for "without water") people settled this little oasis a thousand years ago. Using available limestone rocks, the Sinagua built small rooms into alcoves in the canyon walls, covering the stones with mud plaster to seal out the drafts and perhaps to improve the appearance of their dwellings. It would only be a guess, but all indications point to a hospitable life for the ancient people who lived in Walnut Canyon. Not much reminds you of the 21st century—or even the interstate highway not far away.

"Our television can go here, the couch here, and this one could be my room." Kids quickly get into imagining furnishing the prehistoric rooms, even if their furniture is from more contemporary times. Conditions were a little more cramped than today's youngsters might imagine. One family usually shared a single room, but the rooms were mostly for sleeping since the requirements for tending crops, grinding corn, and hunting for game consumed most of the daylight hours.

After completing the loop trail, you find yourself at the base of the 240 steps leading back to the rim. The solitude of the canyon, broken only by the sounds of birds, including the descending notes of the canyon wren, almost creates the sense of an island paradise worthy of Robinson Crusoe. It is with slight hesitation that you leave this special little canyon. It would be a pleasant experience to spend the night—or even a couple days—listening to the sound of the wind washing over the trees and perhaps capture the spirit of the people who once called this place home more than 1,000 years ago.

In a cycle repeated all over the Southwest, the ancient Sinagua people at Walnut Canyon flourished for more than 300 years and then vanished. Much of the evidence gathered so far suggests that drought was the principle reason people gradually drifted away. They may have been seeking more reliable sources of water.

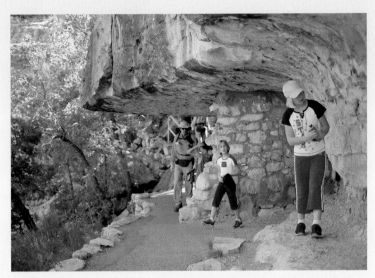

Ledges carved into the canyon walls by Walnut Creek provided excellent shelter for about 700 ancient Sinagua, who created small rooms by building stone walls. The fingerprints of the builders were found in the soft mud that covered the stones.

Crypto Scene

The geology beneath our feet controls many more aspects of our lives than we may realize. It quite literally sets the stage upon which later events unfold. Prehistoric cultures provide us with a few examples. The geologic layer of Kaibab Limestone in Walnut Canyon presented its earliest inhabitants with a unique opportunity. Can you guess what that might be?

As Walnut Creek winds its way east and north on its way to the Little Colorado River, it gradually cut its way down through the relatively soft limestone, creating the canyon. At the same time, the water cut sideways along its bank, leaving shallow caves and ledges now perched 150 feet above the streambed as the canyon became deeper. The Sinagua took advantage of the canyon geology, making perfect sites to construct modest-size rooms with minimum effort and constructing rooms that required building only two walls instead of four. With all the Kaibab Limestone rock scattered everywhere, even the construction of the walls became an easy matter. Do you have examples of how geology has influenced your life?

The striking crazy-quilt pattern of Coconino Sandstone comes into view across the canyon from the Island Trail. Windblown sand deposited 265 million years ago was gradually compressed into the rock we see today.

Can you guess why the south-facing alcoves were the first used for room construction? The angle of the sun during the winter months provided extra warmth to the inhabitants. That meant cutting less firewood each winter and made for pleasant afternoons enjoying the sunshine. The early cultures were keenly aware of the world around them, taking full advantage of the existing resources and conditions of their environment.

Pick up a piece of Kaibab Limestone, a sedimentary rock formation deposited under a shallow inland sea about 250 million years ago. The rock evolved from crushed shells of small sea creatures such as corals, snails, and clams, cemented together under heat and pressure. A careful examination with a hand lens will confirm its origins. The canyon rim and Island Trail route are both limestone.

Once you are on the Island Trail, look into the canyon, especially on the west and northwest walls, and you will see the distinctive Coconino Sandstone Formation, below the Kaibab layer. Another sedimentary rock, Coconino Sandstone results from the gradual accumulation of windblown tiny quartz sand grains. You can easily see a jumble of layers, called *cross bedding*, which resulted from shifting wind patterns along the ancient shallow sea or subsequent lake. Deposited at a different angle, the layers remained undisturbed for centuries as they solidified. Coconino Sandstone, deposited about 265 million years ago, contains no fossil remains, but occasionally tracks from invertebrates and reptiles are visible. If you visit the Grand Canyon, both the Kaibab and Coconino formations are evident.

Crypto Scene

After spending time in Walnut Canyon, the average visitor comes away with a very personal experience and insight into the daily lives of a people not much different from us. The small community of rooms represents many families, each seeking to establish a fulfilling life. Walnut Canyon is also a jumping off point for exploring cultural differences. As with so many educational journeys, respect comes from understanding both the cultural differences and the similarities between our ways of life.

Cultural Bridges

Exhibits produced from decades of geologic and archeological research conducted by the Museum of Northern Arizona provide the most comprehensive presentation of the region's prehistory. Located north of Flagstaff on US 180, the Museum of Northern Arizona is well worth adding to your visit to the Flagstaff area.

During the summer months, the museum sponsors several cultural programs that focus on American Indians of the Southwest, especially the Navajo and Hopi tribes. Demonstrations of weaving, pottery making, and silverwork are a few of the special programs offered to museum guests. Understanding the artistic expressions of tribal members presents insights into their way of life. For example, the katsina dolls, carved by the Hopi, are part of a sacred tradition. The katsina is a supernatural being who lives on the San Francisco Peaks that dominate the Flagstaff skyline. The role of the katsina in the Hopi world is that of a messenger who carries the prayers of the people to their gods.

The Arizona black walnut tree was a valuable source of food and dye to the ancient inhabitants of the canyon. Look for the grayish-brown bark of mature walnut trees along the trail.

Art is not separate from the rest of American Indian life, but a part of it. Among the Pueblo people, such as the Hopi, their language does not have a word for art—or even artist. The American Indian people view the world around them in a unique fashion. Their relationship with the natural world is crucial. This is especially true in establishing a sense of "place." Their strength and sense of well-being are one with the land. The Hopi are descendants of the Sinagua people of Walnut Canyon and other locations around northern Arizona. Hopi have walked this ground for hundreds of years.

If you were an advance scout for the Sinagua, what would you look for in a future house site? Would you be looking for reliable water sources? How about flat land for growing crops? No doubt the early reports coming back about the Walnut Canyon area were encouraging and it is conceivable that a small group of Sinagua decided to commit to settling the area. Archeologists concluded that the first inhabitants of the area lived in small, often single-room, pit houses on the rim above the canyon. Tree-ring dating shows that around A.D. 1125, rainfall in the region increased. The increase in rainfall, coupled with the deposits of fine volcanic ash from the eruption of Sunset Crater (see p. 154) in 1064, combined to make the land more productive. Increased construction activity at Walnut Canyon coincided with the increased rain and volcanic activity.

The eruption of Sunset Crater plays an important role in the prehistoric cultures of northern Arizona. The Sinagua who lived near Walnut Canyon were relatively few at first. Within a couple of decades of the volcanic eruption, however, their numbers started to grow and their trade routes both north and south expanded. Ideas as well as goods traveled these routes, as reflected in changes in architectural styles and construction techniques, and perhaps in manner of dress and self-adornment. It may not have been the information superhighway, but ancient trade routes did significantly contribute to the exchange of ideas and products, resulting in the gradual advancement of civilization.

The Museum of Northern Arizona in Flagstaff displays artifacts found at Walnut Canyon and other Sinagua sites in northern Arizona, as well as contemporary Indian arts and crafts. The museum makes an excellent addition to your explorations of the prehistoric past and the geology of the region.

Farming the open meadows along the rim of the canyon, the Sinagua then lowered their food by rope in pottery jars and baskets over the canyon rim to their houses below for storage for the coming winter months. Evidence suggests the Sinagua built small check dams along Walnut Creek as impoundments for irrigation and as places to collect drinking water. While water may have been slightly more abundant than today, the discovery of a 35-gallon clay pots suggests that, even then, it was still a precious commodity. Carried by hand from the creek below or lowered from the rim above, every drop must have been important. Do you think kids had to carry water as a household chore? If so, it would give a completely new meaning to "household chores," and may eliminate any reason to complain about taking out the trash, which the Sinagua probably just tossed into the canyon. What is trash to most people is a valuable source of information to archeologists, since they often contain the discarded implements used in everyday living, such as broken pottery, bones from animals used for food, seeds from plants, worn sandals, and clothing. What was garbage for the Sinagua is gold to the archeologist.

Carrying shovels, pick axes, and even dynamite, souvenir hunters plundered the ruins of the Sinagua, almost destroying them. Knocking down walls to let in more light, they thoughtlessly stole pottery, baskets, woven sandals, pieces of fabric, and arrowheads. For archeologists, these items reveal volumes of information about the Sinagua. Without a written language, only the artifacts of their daily lives survive to help us understand who they were and how they lived. Fortunately, a few individuals were able to view the past and the future at the same time, and initiated an effort to set aside the ruins as a national park site. The ability to look at the past, present, and future remains a critical trait for people to nurture. Look for the ways, big and small, that you can enrich the lives of future generations just as others have enriched your life by enabling you to visit and enjoy Walnut Canyon National Monument.

Travel Log

- Walnut Canyon National Monument contact information: nps.gov/waca, 928-526-3367.
- Walnut Canyon is 10 miles east of Flagstaff on I-40 at exit 204. Drive 3 miles to Canyon Rim.
- A pair of binoculars is helpful when viewing ruins across the canyon and for spotting bird life in the canyon.
- Bring a small hand lens for examining rock specimens.
- For your rock collection: Look for Kaibab Limestone or Coconino Sandstone, two representative rock types from this area. Check local rock shops in Flagstaff for samples.

18

White Mountains

One of the best ways to escape the heat of summer is to head for the White Mountains of eastern Arizona, where you can camp, hike, fish, bike, watch wildlife, and ride horseback while surrounded by high peaks and lush forests.

Just getting to the White Mountains can be a memorable experience. Between Globe and Show Low, breathtaking US 60 coils back and forth like a snake in its steep descent across Salt River Canyon. A popular tubing waterway farther downstream, the river here marks the boundary between the San Carlos Apache and Fort Apache Indian Reservations. From the rest area overlooking the river, you can walk across a pedestrian bridge next to the Salt River Canyon Bridge, a colorful 380-foot span that features art designed by the two Apache Indian tribes.

Venturing into the White Mountains from Clifton or Eagar on US 191 takes you along the Coronado Trail Scenic Byway, named for the Spanish explorer who traveled this route in 1540. Relentlessly twisting and turning up the rugged backbone of the mountains from the enormous gouge of Morenci Mine in the south, this spectacular road must be the slowest route in the West. Still, this part of the Coronado Trail offers some of the best views in the region from the mammoth copper mining operation above Clifton to beautiful Blue Vista Overlook on the Mogollon Rim. Perched at 9,184 feet, Blue Vista puts you on top of the world, where views of 10,000-foot peaks and upper Sonoran Desert roll away in every direction.

Show Low, Springerville, Eagar, and Alpine offer all the comforts of civilization for those starting out on or returning from an adventure in the White Mountains. Each town features a U.S. Forest Service Ranger Station, an essential place to obtain updates on current conditions and information about one of the most exciting activities in the White Mountains—discovering a rare Mexican gray wolf in the wild.

"Just about everyone you talk to around here has seen a wolf," says a Forest Service employee at the Alpine Ranger Station. "You can see them crossing the road or hunting for rodents. Early morning hours are best." Visitors to the ranger station can inquire about the condition of the reintroduced wolf population in the National Forest wolf recovery area and learn

Wildlife watchers can view golden and bald eagles, swans, and geese, while anglers may catch rainbow, cutthroat, and brook trout at Luna Lake, which sits 7,900 feet above sea level just east of Alpine.

where recent sightings have occurred. Adding the possibility of a wolf sighting to your hiking or camping experience makes any trip to the White Mountains especially exciting.

Wild Things

"We see them here pretty often, running and jumping around out in the open," says a woman at Hannagan Meadow Lodge. Situated 22 miles south of Alpine in a postcard-perfect mountain setting, the rustic 1926 inn offers meals and rooms in the heart of wildlife watching country. In summer, hummingbirds buzz around on a big porch that faces a sea of green grass that serves as a salad bar to elk. Black bear, deer, coyotes, and bobcats also visit Hannagan Meadow, but Mexican gray wolves often provide the most thrilling experience with their nighttime howls and their morning romps in the meadows. "They look like they're just out there to have fun," says the woman. "Sometimes they're not hunting at all. They're just out there playing like kids."

Before the early 1900s, Mexican gray wolves, also called lobos, were common in these forests as well as in western New Mexico, western Texas,

In the White Mountains, watch for eye-catching signs identifying Mexican gray wolf recovery areas. Additional signage helps visitors understand wolf behavior and how to travel safely in wolf country.

Observing wolves in the wild is a thrilling experience, but remember to maintain a safe distance. As when watching all wildlife, use binoculars and long telephoto lenses to view the animal's natural behavior with minimum disturbance.

photo courtesy of George Andrejko, Arizona Game and Fish Department

and northern Mexico. With the expansion of human settlements, their prey decreased and increased livestock herds attracted predators. Conflicts between wolves and ranchers prompted the federal government to destroy wolves until only a few remained in the mid-1900s. Until recently, the last report of a Mexican gray wolf seen in the United States occurred in 1970, and the last recorded observation in Mexico was in 1980.

A Howling Success

Mexico joined the United States in a recovery effort in 1976 when Mexican gray wolves were listed as an endangered species. Biologists captured wolves in Mexico and started a captive breeding population. Eleven Mexican gray wolves were transferred to large enclosures in remote areas of the National Forest in 1998. After a few weeks of adjusting to their new surroundings, the lobos were released and free to roam 7,000 square miles of designated recovery area in Arizona and New Mexico. Since that time, biological monitoring has shown that the wolves are able to survive in the wild, reproduce, and raise pups. Field data such as sightings, tracks, and howling, combined with data from radio collar monitoring, show that more than 50 wolves now live in the recovery area.

Blue Range Wolf Recovery Area signs may be seen throughout the Apache and Gila National Forests in Arizona and New Mexico. Take time to read one of these informative signs to learn about wolf behavior and understand how to act in wolf habitat. Travel slowly to increase your chances of observing wolves and keep pets under control at all times. View all wildlife from a distance to better observe their natural behavior—and never feed wild animals. Wolves are generally cautious of humans and will not threaten people. As one hiker in near Hannagan Meadow says, "We shared the trail with a group of wolves the other day. They were curious, but shy, and went on their way."

Micro Scape

Expansive forests cloak the White Mountains, inviting desert dwellers to enjoy high-country shade when temperatures in Phoenix and Tucson creep up past 100 degrees. Cool air and ample moisture produce thick spruce-fir, aspen, and mixed conifer forests, making the many area campgrounds great places to find shade and privacy. However, the ponderosa pine forests of the White Mountains are particularly impressive, not just for their stately appearance, but because they are part of the largest ponderosa pine forest on the continent, extending 200 miles west to Flagstaff!

Atop the Mogollon Rim, ponderosa pine forests grow in almost unmixed stands that cover thousands of acres. What makes these trees unique is their ability to live with fire. Ponderosa pines have evolved to thrive in regions with mild winters, dry springs, and warm summer storms accompanied by lightning. Historically, this climate allowed low-intensity fires sparked by lightning to quickly burn the surface of grassy ponderosa woodlands, clearing debris and releasing seeds from pine cones. Mature ponderosas with thick bark can resist such surface fires, but shrubs and seedling trees cannot survive, creating an open, park-like atmosphere. This repeating cycle produced vigorous ponderosa pine forests with immense cinnamon-barked trees and open grassy meadows. With increased human settlement, grazing away of grasslands, and changing attitudes toward fire, this natural sequence was interrupted. Each time a fire was extinguished to protect personal property or prevent a larger wildfire, more trees were allowed to grow, creating dense forests of thin trees. Many open woodlands have turned into forests of matchsticks ready for destructive wildfires to strike.

As you travel in the White Mountains, you may see evidence of fire in the blackened snags of dead trees or the lush growth of new plants reclaiming the darkened soil. Although forest managers are working to reverse the decades of overgrowth with prescribed fire, thinning, and timber harvests, much work remains and the risk of uncontrolled fire still exists. Hiking in the ponderosa pine forests of the White Mountains is a good way to understand the role of fire in nature. Compare an open, grassy, ponderosa pine woodland to a dense ponderosa forest crowded with spindly trees. Which area seems like better wildlife habitat? Which ponderosa pines are your grandchildren likely to see?

Whether you are on a remote backpacking excursion or enjoying an overnight stay, tent camping is a favorite activity in the White Mountains. The Hannagan Meadow Campground, less than 0.5 mile south of the lodge of the same name, offers secluded camping in a high-elevation forest, as well as convenient access to the Acker Lake Trail and remote areas of the Blue Range.

Travel Log

- White Mountains contact information: whitemtns.com.

- Consult a detailed map for specific driving directions to the many destinations scattered throughout the White Mountains.

- A good hub for activities, Show Low—named for the winning hand in a card game—is a modern, bustling town surrounded by the extensive forests of the White Mountains. From Tucson, head northeast on AZ 77 to US 60, a total of about 190 miles; from Phoenix, travel east on US 60, a distance of 175 miles; and from Flagstaff, drive east on I-40 and head southeast on AZ 77 for a total of 138 miles.

- To reach the more remote, but classic, mountain town of Alpine from Tucson, head northeast on AZ 77 to US 60, then travel south on US 191 for a total of about 264 miles; from Phoenix, travel east on US 60, then south on US 191 for a total distance of 248 miles; and from Flagstaff, drive east on I-40 and head southeast on AZ 77 before traveling south on US 191 for a total of 210 miles.

- The changing seasons of Arizona's White Mountains present outstanding year-round recreational opportunities, including cross-country skiing and other winter activities. The area also offers a taste of pioneer history dating back to the late 1800s when Mormon settlers established agriculture and timber industries. Visit the small communities of Pinetop, Lakeside, Greer, Snowflake, and Taylor to discover each town's rural charm and character.

Blackened forests south of Hannagan Meadow along US 191 are evidence of a 2004 wildfire. Decades of fire prevention have resulted in dense stands of thin trees which increase the danger of destructive wildfires.

19

Wupatki and Sunset Crater Volcano National Monuments

Discovery Zone

A prehistoric apartment house stands just behind the visitor center at Wupatki National Monument! Four stories high, with more than 100 rooms, it was home to more than 200 people almost 1,000 years ago. *Wupatki,* which means "tall house" in the Hopi language, stands silent today except for an occasional gust of wind that long ago carried away the voices of its inhabitants. Two other structures immediately capture your attention—a circular plaza stands in the foreground and, off to the right, an oval-shaped, doubled-walled structure with vertical slots at both ends. What purpose did they serve to the ancient people who lived here? Indeed, who lived here? Why did they find this isolated location so appealing?

The variety of discoveries at Wupatki National Monument allows modern-day explorers a chance to build a bridge between today's world and the prehistoric one—because it is before local recorded history. Everything you discover along the trail and in the museum are pieces of the puzzle. The architecture, artifacts, and even the trash left behind by the early inhabitants contribute to reconstructing a way of life that has vanished.

More than 2,600 individual prehistoric dwellings exist in the 56 square miles of Wupatki National Monument. Mystery and speculation surround the Citadel Ruin; almost fortress-like in appearance, it stands guard above a geologic sinkhole north and west of Wupatki. No other dwelling in the Wupatki area exhibits such defensive construction. Each of the five ancient pueblos open to the public is unique, but soon your eye will detect the ruins of many other dwellings that dot the landscape.

To appreciate these ancient people, you need to sense the invisible strings that tie the early inhabitants of the Wupatki Basin together. Seasonal ceremonies, perhaps in the oval-shaped ball court at Wupatki, bound the society together. Imagine walking from your home to visit a friend or a relative, perhaps to carry a meal or a gift to a family member. These ruins may now seem abandoned and even neglected, but they once were vibrant with people going about the daily business of living.

The prehistoric four-story Wupatki Pueblo contained about 100 rooms. It may have served as a ceremonial center for a larger area, with an open-air amphitheater and ball court adjacent to the pueblo.

Look carefully up the wash to the left and behind the Wupatki Pueblo. Do you see the thin traces of black sand against the red? The black sand is all that remains of the volcanic ash that once blanketed the area. Do you see any evidence of agriculture—maybe hints of terraces? Inhabitants probably farmed the wash behind the pueblo, growing crops of squash, corn, and beans. Relying on the rains to encourage growth, early farmers benefited from the thin covering of volcanic ash that settled over the land following the eruption of the Sunset Crater volcano. Take a journey along the paved trail through this ancient neighborhood.

Paleo Scene

What is the connection between Wupatki and the eruption of Sunset Crater? Volcanic ash from the eruption actually set the stage for the growth of prehistoric populations in the Wupatki Basin. Drifting across an area almost 800 square miles in size, the ash acted as mulch, retaining the sparse moisture that falls in this dry high desert. It permitted the growing of crops in areas that might not otherwise support agriculture. The moisture-retaining capacity of the ash allowed for better growth and warmed the seeds in the early stages of growth.

Sunset Crater erupted in 1064. Continuing intermittently for almost 200 years, the eruptions eventually created a new volcanic cinder cone. Early explorers gave the crater its name because of the reddish-tinged volcanic cinders around its peak. The mountain grew to a height of 1,000 feet, but was only the latest volcano to form in one of the largest volcanic fields in North America. To the west, Humphreys Peak, the tallest at 12,643 feet high, is part of the San Francisco Mountains volcanic field.

Cinder cones are only one type of volcano. Their formation occurs by explosive eruptions, which throw large volumes of ash and cinders high into the air. The heaviest of the volcanic cinders fall directly down around the eruption vent, gradually building up a mound, almost like a sand pile. After the eruptions subsided, word gradually spread among the prehistoric people of the increased agricultural productivity caused by the volcanic ash. A prehistoric land rush occurred rapidly, covering the region with small pueblos.

Crypto Scene

Take the short walk to explore the ball court and the small concrete box adjacent to it. If you are visiting in the afternoon, the chances of feeling a cool breeze flowing out of the box are good. What could it be? Was it prehistoric air conditioning?

Actually, no evidence exists that the prehistoric people knew of its existence. Before it was covered by the box for protection, the blowhole was only a small, stone-lined crevice. This blowhole is one of several found in the region and, in all likelihood, all are connected to an underground space with an estimated volume of 7 billion cubic feet.

The blowhole is a natural phenomenon resulting from the creation of solution cracks and crevices in the Kaibab Limestone, beneath the surrounding red Moenkopi Sandstone. Occasionally, the cracks lead to the surface, allowing for an exchange of air into and out of the underground space. Typically, cooler, denser air flows into the blowhole during the night and in the morning hours and then flows out in the afternoon hours, interrupted by a brief equilibrium during the middle of the day. The flow rates can be very impressive, clocked at 30 miles per hour and able to suspend small objects over the exit hole!

Wild Things

Fleet-footed pronghorn inhabit the grasslands in the northwest portion of the monument. One good viewing location is atop the Citadel Ruin looking to the north. The gazelle-like animals are more frequently observed early and late in the day, but also move about during the day. They are capable of running up to 40 miles per hour and like to try to race ahead of vehicles so

Sometimes called a breathing well or blowhole, these cracks in the earth are connected to a subterranean system of small caves and crevices in limestone. Higher barometric pressures during the late evening and early morning hours forces air into the underground chambers. The flow of air reverses in the afternoon, with the cool morning air flowing out with enough force to float a hat.

they can cross in front. Pronghorn possess exceptional eyesight. Wave a white handkerchief, even at a distance, and they will often look your way. Their curiosity may even cause them to move a little closer. Look for the pronghorn both north and south of the entrance to Wupatki on US 89.

Micro Scape

Investigating prehistoric structures is the principle work of archeologists. Piecing together the evidence offers interesting challenges and frequently combines several scientific disciplines in recreating history.

The science of *dendrochronology*, or tree-ring dating, is an invaluable tool for building a bridge to the past. Most people know that as trees grow, they add an annual ring of growth to their diameter. The ring is either wide or narrow depending on the amount of growth that occurs within a given year. A year with little or no rainfall produces a very narrow ring. Conversely, a year with a lot of rain results in more growth and a wider ring. When scientists examined cross sections of logs used in the construction of prehistoric pueblos, they observed patterns of wet and dry cycles in annual growth rings. The rings in the prehistoric dwellings, however, represent an isolated piece of information, disconnected to the present.

Dr. A.E. Douglass, considered the "Father of Dendrochronology," reasoned that by examining the tree-ring patterns from tree stumps of the same species, he could gradually work his way backwards by matching tree-ring patterns in older and older trees. Douglass was successful and he was eventually able to reconstruct a path to the past. Dendrochonology indicated that construction of the Wupatki Pueblo began in 1130.

Modern dendrochronology uses the Swedish *increment borer*, a metal tube, to obtain core samples from living trees, which allows scientists to obtain the growth-ring history, building the bridge to the past. Through the development of this highly valuable research technique, archeologists were able to determine the exact year in which a log was cut for use in the construction of the prehistoric dwelling. This information also provides a glimpse of the available moisture during the same period.

Back in Time Line

The earliest inhabitants of the region, the Sinagua, were a relatively primitive people who lived in "pit houses," so named because the clay floors of their houses were below ground level. Their society was relatively undeveloped. The eruption of Sunset Crater prompted the arrival of new cultures that heavily influenced the Sinagua.

Ideas move with people. With the arrival of each new family, society in the Wupatki Basin evolved. Wupatki became a multicultural center, reflecting cultural elements from several points on the compass. The more advanced ancestral Puebloan people (from northeast of Wupatki) provided knowledge for the construction of above-ground masonry houses. The Hohokam people, migrating up from the Salt and Gila Valleys to the south, brought with them the knowledge of irrigation techniques. The Cohonina, Prescott, and Mogollon people all contributed new ideas and each group brought with them their distinctive pottery.

Pieces of the Past

The abundance and variety of *potsherds*, or broken pieces of pottery, in and around the prehistoric dwellings provide an important insight into the changing social fabric of the Wupatki Basin following the eruption of Sunset Crater. Black-on-White, Grey Ware, Red-On-Buff, Polychrome, and Black-on-Orange are just a few of the many decorative styles of pottery uncovered. The sheer amount of pottery suggests that, in addition to trading with nearby cultures, people permanently migrated into the Wupatki Basin to seek a better life and new opportunities.

Archeologists discovered jewelry, small copper bells, turquoise, textiles, leather, and seashells in burial sites, inside the rooms within the pueblo, and often in the trash mounds or kitchen middens close to their dwellings. Each object not known to the early Sinagua people led archeologists to another point on the compass to establish the routes of trade between the prehistoric cultures. More recently, researchers discovered pieces of volcanic rock with

Mystery surrounds the amphitheater or dance plaza. Archeologists are uncertain about its exact use and, because timbers were not used in its construction, precise dating is not possible.

Sacred to the Hopi and Navajo people, the snowcapped San Francisco Peaks in the distance are part of the second-largest volcanic field in North America.

impressions of corncobs. Speculation suggests that the early Sinagua placed corncobs near still-hot lava as either an offering or a type of charm to ensure good fortune or protection from the volcano. No one is certain what prompted the practice. As you walk in the ancient pathways of Wupatki ruins, keep a sharp eye out for these pieces of the past. Remember, it is against the law to remove these objects and, more importantly, they will enrich the experience of those visitors who follow.

Many mysteries surround the inhabitants of Wupatki. You might even be able to solve one or two yourself. One such unanswered question is the T-shaped doorway found at stop 16 along the Wupatki Ruins Trail. The unusual doorway shape is common to many prehistoric dwellings through-out the Southwest. Do you have any ideas about why they would construct such a door shape?

What was the function of the circular plaza, which was sometimes called an amphitheater or dance plaza? Some speculate that it might have been an open-air ceremonial plaza, similar to a kiva. Common to many prehistoric pueblos, a kiva is usually covered. The kiva has a *sipapu,* or "spirit hole," through which the spirits of the underworld entered into the kiva during ceremonies. The circular plaza at Wupatki had no evidence of being covered or having a sipapu. Was Wupatki a ceremonial center for the people of the surrounding pueblos?

The ball court presents the greatest mystery. The remains of Hohokam villages still visible in the area of modern Phoenix, feature several ball courts. The Hohokam people must have brought the idea of the ball court with them, along with their well-developed culture, to their new life at Wupatki.

- Wupatki National Monument contact information: nps.gov/wupa, 928-679-2365.

- Sunset Crater Volcano National Monument contact information: nps.gov/sucr, 928-526-0502.

- The loop road that provides access to Wupatki and Sunset Crater Volcano National Monuments is 12 miles north of Flagstaff on US 89. Enter the loop road at Sunset Crater and drive to Wupatki.

- An interesting stop, if you continue north along the loop road back to US 89 and turn south back to Flagstaff, is a visit to the Sacred Mountain Trading Post. This is not your typical convenience store, although snacks and pop are available. It is still an active trading post. The trading post was often the principal method for American Indians to obtain limited groceries and other necessities, plus an outlet for selling their pottery, rugs, and jewelry. Trading posts often provided a place to catch up on news and gossip. If you can afford the time to slow down a bit, the trading post offers a glimpse into the past. Visiting with the post trader on the pottery, jewelry, baskets, and occasional blankets offered for sale helps gain some insight into the way of life on the reservation.

- Do not pick up pieces of the past. Potsherds, while seemingly abundant, are part of the archeological resources at Wupatki. Federal law protects them along with all other historic and prehistoric artifacts. Leave them as you found them.

- A good energy-burner early in the day is the self-guided trail at Sunset Crater Volcano National Monument. The trail provides excellent insight into volcanic features and provides for that all-important "let's get out and do something" activity. Watch out for sharp lava rock, and be sure to wear sturdy shoes.

- A quick study of the Indian Country map offers many alluring side-trip destinations, often on unimproved roads. Make local inquiries about road conditions and be sure to include sufficient water and snacks in the event that a sudden summer thunderstorm closes the roads.

- For your rock collection: Look for lava and Moenkopi sandstone, but collect samples outside protected areas.

20

Yuma

Discovery Zone

Cross the desert at Yuma and become connected to American Indians, Spanish explorers, steamboat captains, miners, and others who passed this way long ago. Scenes from a varied history lie in every direction from two massive granite outcroppings that mark a centuries-old route. A sturdy mission church adorns the hilltop to the north, while an expansive guard tower stands sentry to the south. Vehicles occupy a steel truss bridge, flanked by trains traveling on time-tested tracks. Below flows the force that links them all: the enduring Colorado River.

Take a boat trip on the meandering Colorado River just northeast of Yuma to encounter clues about the area's history. "This river once ran like a chocolate milkshake," recounts Captain Ron Knowlton as he guides visitors on a jet-boat tour through the Imperial Wildlife Refuge. "It was too thick to drink and too thin to plow," he continues as he describes the character of the Colorado before construction of the Laguna Dam in 1907. In the past, free-flowing water would flood low-lying areas, leaving behind sand and silt that created rich farmland.

From Steamboats to Speedboats

On your way to the Eureka Mining District, you can imagine Captain George Johnson steering one of the first paddleboats from Yuma in 1853, unloading freight and taking on firewood at landings along the Colorado. Named the "General Jesup," Johnson's side-wheeler was part of the Colorado Steam Navigation Company fleet, a financial success that opened remote regions of Arizona to trade and travel.

It is easy to get lost in history here, but expect a cooling splash from the wake of an occasional speedboat to bring you back to the present. High above a multihued ridge studded with intriguing petroglyphs, a stately bighorn ram scans the stony landscape below. Watchman's Cabin becomes visible between two tall crags in the distance. From this small rock fortress, a lookout could see steam from paddleboats two days away. Signals were sent by mirror to another communication station at Picacho Peak to announce the approach of oncoming river traffic.

Hikers investigate petroglyphs on a rocky ridge called "the billboard" alongside the Colorado River near Yuma. Pecked into the rocks hundreds of years ago, mysterious abstract designs appear alongside human shapes and animal figures.

Slowly prodding its way through a jungle tunnel of cane and cattails, the jet boat comes to rest on the riverbank near a trail that leads to an 1880s mining cabin. Boaters scramble around on rocks, examining specimens of quartz and mica. Some rest in rocking chairs on the rickety porch, while others quiz the guide about resident wildlife. Watching from atop a big boulder, a burly chuckwalla bids the passengers good-bye as the boat continues upriver toward Picacho Peak State Park.

Passing the old Picacho stamp mill brings to mind images of the Old West. Millions of dollars in gold were once mined in these hills, supporting a town of 2,500 people, three saloons, and a general store. Although some private mining still occurs at the site, local residents now seem limited to a few snowy egrets. After a quick break at a state park boat-in campground to use the restrooms and read some interpretive signs, the jet boat takes passengers to Norton's Landing for lunch and more history. Equipped with ramadas and picnic tables, a knoll at the site overlooks a broad expanse of water, cattails, and mesquite trees. Hummingbirds, flycatchers, and warblers dart around as visitors pick through interesting rock samples and artifacts of life on the river. A box of historic photos shows great hustle and bustle here as silver and lead ore from the Red Cloud Mine was loaded onto steamboats bound for Yuma and beyond. Servicing more than 100 area mine claims, Norton's Steamboat Landing was once the largest town on the river.

Returning downriver, a few wild burros can be seen trudging along in the wildlife refuge. One last stop at a petroglyph site called "the billboard" offers a chance to imagine life along the river in yet another bygone era. Ancient images of humans, birds, and puzzling spirals have been pecked

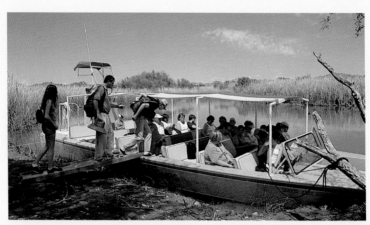

Passengers board a boat on the Colorado River north of Yuma at Norton's Landing, once the site of a thriving 1800s mining town.

from the surfaces of these rocks for some mysterious purpose. You will want to linger and try to decode the primitive language of pictures until the hot midday sun signals that it is time to return to the cool, shimmering water— back to the ribbon of life called the Colorado.

Crypto Scene

The Red Cloud Mine north of Yuma produced thousands of dollars in lead and silver by 1890, but the discovery of the mineral wulfenite in the 1880s would eventually bring an entirely new meaning to the idea of rock hounding in Yuma County.

A geologic fault in the Red Cloud Mine possesses a vein of volcanic rock featuring cavities and cracks lined with wulfenite crystals. The brilliant red-orange color and the unusual size and perfect shape of wulfenite from this mine make it some of the finest in the world. Collectors have been fascinated with the Red Cloud wulfenite since 1938, when some of the most outstanding specimens ever unearthed received worldwide attention. In 2000, a group of professional miners reopened an area of the Red Cloud Mine known to contain wulfenite. Three years of hard work in the scorching desert finally revealed a gem pocket of translucent crystals just as the miners were about to give up their quest. The number of wulfenite specimens was as exceptional as the fine quality of the crystals found. Although the miners continued excavating for a while, no additional wulfenite was discovered and the mine was closed for reclamation late in 2003.

Wild Things

Migrating birds literally flock to Yuma in spring and fall, when the Colorado River Valley offers lush, green habitat to more than 380 species traveling along the Pacific flyway migratory pattern. Birding locations abound, from Mittry Lake Wildlife Area to the easily accessible community West Wetlands, where even novice wildlife watchers can spot American redstarts as well as a variety of warblers and hummingbirds. Waterfowl and shorebirds are effortless to observe during winter when Canada geese, canvasbacks, and even sandhill cranes call Yuma home. Once you get hooked on identifying these species, you will want to attend the annual Yuma Birding and Nature Festival. Held at the height of spring, this popular event includes field trips, presentations, and activities for all bird enthusiasts.

Back in Time Line

Visit Yuma Crossing State Historic Park to better connect the cultural dots of changing communities along the Colorado River. The park's film and exhibits reveal how the river was the center of life for the Quechan, Cocopah, and Mohave tribes, who relied on floodwaters to nourish their plantings of beans, corn, and squash in the otherwise barren desert soil. Before the Colorado River was dammed, it could become 15 miles wide during periodic floods. This made the narrow gap between the two granite outcroppings one of the few places to conveniently cross the river. From their strategic location on the bluffs above, the Quechan (once called the Yuma) could observe travelers approaching from the Pacific Coast or from the east.

Yuma Crossing proved an important trade route not only for the Quechan, but for later explorers and settlers as well. The first non-American Indian to encounter the crossing was Spaniard Hernando de Alarçon, who sailed up the Colorado River in 1540 to provide supplies for the Coronado expedition. Mountain men and gold seekers followed. When Yuma became a territorial possession of the United States in 1849, the U.S. Army took control of Quechan lands to establish Fort Yuma.

Step into the Office of the Quartermaster and transport yourself to a time when the depot stored supplies for military posts in Utah, Nevada, New Mexico, and throughout Arizona. Goods—such as clothing, food, and ammunition—found their way to Yuma after being hauled on ships from California and around the Baja Peninsula to Port Isabel at the mouth of the Colorado River. Steamboats carried the cargo upstream to Yuma, where it was unloaded and stocked in an oversize central storehouse, before distribution by paddleboat upriver or mule-drawn wagons inland. When you enter the storehouse, climb the steps of the steamboat display and take your place at the helm of a 19th-century paddle wheeler. Imagine navigating through sandbars and snags hauling tons of freight up the untamed waters of the Colorado River!

Freight trains ended the riverboat era when the Southern Pacific Railroad reached Yuma in 1877. As a result, the supply depot closed in 1883. Exhibits throughout the state park depict these many transitions, including customs operations and underwater work accomplished by the Bureau of Reclamation. A view of the Ocean-to-Ocean highway bridge that was built next to the railroad bridge in 1915 can be seen from many places in the park, reminding visitors of the centuries of change at Yuma Crossing.

Take the helm of a riverboat at Yuma Crossing State Historic Park where you can imagine navigating the colorful Colorado River during its heyday as a commercial waterway. With many historic exhibits, the park is a great place to study Arizona's past.

From 1864 to 1883, steamboats delivered supplies to the Yuma quartermaster depot, where the U.S. Army stored and distributed goods to military posts in the Southwest. Historic buildings and interpretive exhibits at the site are now part of Yuma Crossing State Historic Park. Photo courtesy of Arizona State Parks

Completed in 1915, the Ocean-to-Ocean highway bridge at Yuma Crossing allowed trains to enter Arizona from the west.

Travel Log

- Yuma contact information: yumacity.com
- Yuma is located along I-8, 240 miles from Tucson and 170 miles from San Diego.
- Elevation is only 138 feet above sea level, so winter temperatures are mild and summer temperatures often exceed 100 degrees. Yuma is the sunniest city in the United States with as many as 339 days of sunshine per year.
- Bring plenty of sunscreen and a hat, especially if you take a trip on the Colorado River. Bring binoculars, a camera, and a birding guide to make the most of your experience.
- Contact the Imperial National Wildlife Refuge at P.O. Box 72217, Yuma, AZ, 85365, 928-783-3371. To visit the refuge headquarters, take US 95 north 22 miles to Martinez Lake Road, turn west, and continue 13 miles. Turn right on a graded gravel road marked Imperial National Wildlife Refuge, and continue 4 miles to refuge headquarters. Ask about boat-in camping opportunities within Picacho State Recreation Area if you are interested in an overnight stay on the river.
- Contact Yuma River Tours at 928-783-4400. Tours are three, five, and seven hours long. Discount packages are available for student field trips. Take US 95 north 22 miles to Martinez Lake Road, turn west, and continue 10 miles to Fisher's Landing, the departure point for all tours.
- In 2000, Yuma Crossing was designated as a national heritage area. Historic sites in Yuma in addition to Yuma Crossing State Historic Park (928-329-0471) include Yuma Territorial Prison State Historic Park (928-783-4771) and the Arizona Historical Society Century House Museum (928-782-1841).
- For your rock collection: The rare mineral wulfenite, from the Red Cloud Mine, would be a prized addition to a rock collection. Don't be too disappointed if you are unable to find a specimen at a local rock shop because it is very, very expensive! A good alternative might be a piece of marine limestone.

Views of boaters, birds, and beaches prompt hikers to stop atop a promontory adorned with petroglyphs to along the Colorado River just north of Yuma. One of many fascinating "rock art" sites in the area, this ridge is known as the "billboard" for its abundance of bold pictures.

Additional Reading

Start your Arizona adventures with research. The administrators of most sites described in this book, as well as the local chambers of commerce, have compiled useful brochures that are readily available at visitor centers or by mail. Most federal agencies offer informative maps that are essential for any visit. Call or write ahead before you start out on your journeys in Arizona.

The authors recommend the following resources:

Birds of the Southwest. John H. Rappole, Texas A&M University Press, College Station, Texas, 2000.

Black Sands, Prehistory in Northern Arizona. Harold S. Colton, University of New Mexico Press, Albuquerque, New Mexico, 1960.

Hohokam, Prehistoric Cultures of the Southwest. Rose Houk, Southwest Parks and Monuments Association, Tucson, Arizona, 1992.

Juan Bautista de Anza National Historic Trail. Don Garate, Southwest Parks and Monuments Association, Tucson, Arizona, 1994.

Kartchner Caverns State Park. Sam Negri, Department of Transportation, State of Arizona, 1998.

The Meteor Crater Story. Dean Smith, Meteor Crater Enterprises, Inc., Flagstaff, Arizona, 1996.

Montezuma Castle National Monument. Susan Lamb, Western National Parks Association, Tucson, Arizona, 2003.

Petrified Forest, The Story Behind the Scenery. Sidney Ash, published by Petrified Forest Museum, Petrified Forest National Park, Arizona, 1985. Produced by KC Publications, Las Vegas, Nevada.

Plants of Arizona. Anne Orth Epple, The Globe Pequot Press, Guilford, Connecticut, 1995.

Roadside Geology of Arizona. Halka Chronic, Mountain Press Publishing Company, Missoula, Montana, 1983.

Roadside History of Arizona. Marshall Trimble, Mountain Press Publishing Company, Missoula, Montana, 2004.

The Sonoran Desert. Christopher L. Helms, KC Publications, Las Vegas, Nevada, 1980.

Walnut Canyon National Monument. Scott Thybony, Southwest Parks and Monuments Association, Tucson, Arizona, 1996.

Wonders of the Pima Air and Space, Titan Missile Museums. Arizona Aerospace Foundation, 1998.

The Authors

James A. Mack and Diane T. Liggett share a strong interest in authentic destinations as well as in the preservation of natural and cultural resources. The authors combine 40 years of experience in natural and cultural history education with numerous awards for the development of special interpretive programs and publications for the National Park Service. Jim received

 a Bachelor of Science Degree in Wildlife Biology from California State University with graduate work at Northern Arizona University. Diane received a Bachelor of Science Degree in Botany from California State Polytechnic University. The Arizona residents are also coauthors of *Real Cool Colorado Places for Curious Kids.*